Horizon

WINTER, 1967 · VOLUME IX, NUMBER 1

A Box Is Not a Home

On page 70 of this issue David Jacobs describes an unusually attractive new plan for mass housing. Habitat, designed my Moshe Safdie for the Montreal Exposition, offers a happy contrast to such vast prisonlike developments as New York's Lefrak City—filing cases for people, standing end on dreary end. Mr. Safdie's scheme stacks the units in an open arrangement reminiscent of a child's block castle. If mass housing is the pattern of the future, this is one of the most promising solutions we have seen.

And yet—is this the way to live? In his autobiography John Stuart Mill recalled as "an important circumstance of my education" the summers he spent in a country house on the grounds of an abbey in Devonshire. "Nothing," he wrote, "contributes more to nourish elevation of sentiments in a people than the large and free character of their habitations. The middle-age architecture, the baronial hall, and the spacious and lofty rooms of the fine old place, so unlike the mean and cramped externals of English middle-class life, gave the sentiment of a larger and freer existence, and were to me a sort of poetic cultivation, aided also by the character of the grounds in which the abbey stood; which were riant and secluded, umbrageous, and full of the sound of falling waters."

Leaving aside the riant grounds, no doubt it is purely nostalgic to wish for this kind of dwelling in an age of wildly expanding populations. No doubt our descendants will have to eat their dinners of fried algae in some little cluster of boxes which they buy, live in, and discard, as they do their automobiles and Coca-Cola cans.

The only question is whether this kind of life does not violate some deep need common to man and many other living creatures. In his fascinating new book *The Territorial Imperative* Robert Ardrey describes the instinct of many animals to stake out a plot of land big enough to raise a family and to defend that plot against all comers. A nesting ground of herring gulls, for instance, is a huge conglomeration of such plots, each precisely bounded and each guarded as jealously as a gold miner's claim. Ardrey believes that territoriality—the need for one's own turf, as they say in Harlem—is one of the basic animal drives, on a par with hunger and sex. If so, one wonders whether any housing complex, however ingenious and attractive, can ever fulfill it.

At one place in this issue (page 14) Paul Brooks bemoans the threatened extinction of the rhinoceros. Elsewhere Sir Harold Macmillan sheds a statesmanlike tear for the joys of life at a ducal country house of forty years ago. It was surely just as inevitable that the Duke of Devonshire

HORIZON is published every three months by American Heritage Publishing Co.. Inc.

PRESIDENT
James Parton

EDITORIAL COMMITTEE
Joseph J. Thorndike, *Chairman*
Oliver Jensen
Richard M. Ketchum

ART DIRECTOR
Irwin Glusker

SENIOR EDITOR, HORIZON
Marshall B. Davidson

Editorial and executive offices:
551 Fifth Avenue, New York, N.Y. 10017.

EDITOR
Joseph J. Thorndike
MANAGING EDITOR: Charles L. Mee, Jr.
ARTICLES EDITOR: Robert Cowley   ART EDITOR: Jane Wilson
ART DIRECTORS: Kenneth Munowitz, Barbara Asch
ASSOCIATE EDITORS: Shirley Tomkievicz, Robert S. Gallagher
ASSISTANT EDITORS: Barbara Klaw, Priscilla Flood
COPY EDITOR: Mary Ann Pfeiffer   *Assistant:* Joan Wilkinson

ADVISORY BOARD: Gilbert Highet, *Chairman*, Frederick Burkhardt, William Harlan Hale, Jotham Johnson, John Walker
EUROPEAN CONSULTING EDITOR: J. H. Plumb, *Christ's College, Cambridge*
EUROPEAN BUREAU: Gertrudis Feliu, *Chief, 11 rue du Bouloi, Paris I*er

HORIZON

A Magazine of the Arts

WINTER, 1967 · VOLUME IX, NUMBER 1

should be driven from his vast estates as that the rhinoceros, roughly his counterpart in the animal kingdom, is now being driven from his. But if

Devonshire   *Rhinoceros*

landed noblemen have largely disappeared, so too have the peasants of northwestern Europe whose lives were so faithfully recorded by Pieter Bruegel (page 22). The bulldozers are marching as relentlessly across the farmlands of Flanders as they are across the Devonshire downs and the Long Island potato fields, leaving row on row of "housing units" behind them. As the pressure of population grows, the housing units crowd closer together and climb on top of one another, like cartons in a warehouse. If we do not relish this prospect of the future, we had better find some solution to the population explosion, and find it soon. Otherwise, it appears, we will all end up in boxes before we are even dead.

J.J.T.

All correspondence about subscriptions should be addressed to: Horizon Subscription Office, 379 West Center St., Marion, Ohio 43301.

    Single Copies: $ 5.00

    Subscriptions: $16.00 per year in the U.S. & Canada; elsewhere, $17.00

Annual indexes for Volumes I–VII are available at $1 each. A cumulative index for Volumes I–V is available at $3. Horizon is also indexed in the *Readers Guide to Periodical Literature*.

The editors welcome contributions but can assume no responsibility for unsolicited material.

Title registered U.S. Patent Office

Second-class postage paid at New York, N.Y., and at additional mailing offices.

COVER: *The Hunters in the Snow*, of which this is a detail, is one of the supreme achievements of the great Netherlandish painter Pieter Bruegel the Elder. It is from a series of landscapes of the seasons painted during 1565 and probably commissioned for the palatial house of the Antwerp connoisseur Niclaes Jonghelinck. There is some doubt as to the original number of paintings in the series, but five still exist; three of them, including this one, are in the Kunsthistoriches Museum in Vienna. The full painting appears in color in an article on Bruegel's life and work beginning on page 22.

THE TRIAL OF JESUS

Was Christ condemned to death by the Jews, as tradition has held for so long, or was he really executed by the Romans as a political offender?

By a strange irony of history, the surest thing known about Jesus of Nazareth is that he was executed by the Romans for sedition against their government in Judaea. The circumstances of Jesus' birth, the length of his public ministry, and the exact content of his teaching are all matters of uncertainty, but the cause of his death is beyond doubt. For the fact that Jesus was crucified as a rebel on the orders of Pontius Pilate, the Roman procurator of Judaea, is attested by all four Gospels, and it is briefly mentioned by the Roman historian Tacitus, writing early in the second century. The witness of the Gospels is especially significant because the fact of the Roman execution of Jesus on such a charge was very embarrassing for the early Christians. Obviously they would never have invented it; indeed, they probably would not have recorded it if the fact had not been so well known.

That the Gospel writers do describe the crucifixion of Jesus, and the events that led up to it, at considerable length is, in fact, the real cause of the mystery that invests the tragic event. For, on analysis, their accounts are found to be inspired by a strong apologetic motive—indeed, they are attempts to explain the embarrassing fact that Jesus was actually executed as a political offender. Because of this apologetic intent, any attempt to elucidate the problem of the Roman condemnation of Jesus must begin with the Gospel evidence.

The pivotal document is the Gospel of Mark, for it is the earliest of the Gospels, and its narrative framework was closely followed by the authors of the Gospels of Matthew and Luke. The Gospel of John, which is later in date, generally reproduces the Markan presentation of the trial and crucifixion of Jesus, though it is more concerned with the theological significance of these events.

One of the earliest representations of Jesus, painted in a catacomb by Roman Christians some three centuries after the Crucifixion, depicts him as a youthful teacher and lawgiver.

The Gospel of Mark represents an innovation in Christian thought and practice. No one had ever before thought of writing a narrative account of the career of Jesus. The reason for this was undoubtedly the fact that the first Christians believed so strongly that Jesus would shortly return from heaven, with supernatural power, to bring the existing world order to an end. In other words, in the three or four decades following the Crucifixion no need had been felt to record the earthly life of Jesus for posterity—because there would be no posterity!

What, then, brought about the change that produced the Gospel of Mark? Clearly we must look for some adequate cause; the change implies a truly profound alteration in the outlook of the primitive Christians. To answer the question we must know the date of the Gospel. Scholars have been accustomed to date it in the period A.D. 65–75. Now, during this decade the Jews revolted against Rome. The revolt had been coming for some time, owing to Roman maladministration and the Jewish conviction, so fervently held, that the people of Israel could pay allegiance to no other lord than Yahweh, the god of Israel. The revolt broke out in A.D. 66, and for the next four years, the life of the Jewish nation was convulsed in war, until final catastrophe overwhelmed it in A.D. 70, when Jerusalem was captured and razed and its famous Temple destroyed by fire.

The effect of this Jewish War upon the infant Christian church was profound. Hitherto the Christian movement had been directed and controlled from Jerusalem, where the original community of apostles and disciples had been established. This community, the Mother Church of Christianity, disappeared as a result of the war. The consequent situation was dangerous and perplexing for Christians elsewhere. Not only had a direct link with the original source of the authority and tradition of their faith been broken, but they faced the very real danger of being regarded by the Roman government as "fellow travelers" with Jewish nationalism. At no

By S. G. F. BRANDON

place was this danger greater than in Rome itself, the capital of the empire that had been so sorely tried by the Jewish revolt. It was for the Christian community in Rome that the Gospel of Mark was originally written.

This fact of the Roman origin of the Markan Gospel is of supreme significance for determining the date of its composition. The question that now faces us, in the light of the preceding considerations, is when, during the period A.D. 65–75, would the need have arisen among the Christians of Rome for a written record of the career of Jesus, seeing that this need had never been felt before? The evidence points to one answer: the need arose out of the situation caused by the Jewish war against Rome.

The a priori probability that this was so finds remarkable confirmation when we examine the Gospel itself. But first we must notice another fact of great importance in this connection. In the year 71 the emperor Vespasian, together with his sons Titus and Domitian, celebrated a splendid triumph in Rome to commemorate their victory over rebel Judaea. The occasion was one of great significance for both the Roman people and the new imperial dynasty of the Flavii. Since the death of Nero in 68, the Roman state had suffered a series of disasters. It had been plunged into civil war shortly after the Jews had revolted. The Jewish War itself had begun with the crushing defeat of a Roman army by the rebels. The

consequences were likely to have been felt afar, for Judaea occupied an important place in the Roman strategical position in the Near East; the country lay athwart the main routes connecting Egypt with Syria. Also, there was a large Jewish population in Mesopotamia likely to make common cause with their Judaean brethren against Rome, a situation that the Parthians in turn could have exploited to invade the Roman provinces. The Romans had, accordingly, been badly frightened by the Jewish War, and they were profoundly grateful to Vespasian, who had both put an end to the civil war and crushed the Jewish rebels.

Their success in the Jewish War was important to Vespasian and his sons, for they were founding a new imperial dynasty. It would obviously be to their advantage to make the most of their victory by impressing the people of Rome with their achievements. Coins were issued commemorating the conquest of Judaea, but it was the triumph that provided the best opportunity for bringing home to the Roman people the magnitude of their victory. We are fortunate in having a detailed account of the triumphal procession from Josephus, the Jewish historian, who had actually served as a general on the Jewish side.* Through the streets of Rome, on the day concerned, the victorious legionaries paraded, with the trophies of their victory and multitudes of

* For Josephus's account of one of the war's episodes, see "Masada" (pages 26 and 27), in the Winter, 1966, issue of HORIZON.

Christ's triumphal entry into Jerusalem is the subject of a miniature (above) in the Rossano Gospel, a fifth- or sixth-century Byzantine manuscript. Also Byzantine is the portrait of Saint Mark (upper right), the author of the earliest Gospel.

Jewish captives. The treasures of the Temple were borne in the triumphal procession, the great Menorah, or seven-branched candelabra, the altar of shewbread, the silver trumpets, and the purple curtains that had veiled the Holy of Holies. A representation of the scene adorns the Arch of Titus in the Forum (see pages 12–13).

This triumph must have made the Jewish revolt very real to the people of Rome; it was designed to render them vividly aware of the gravity of the danger from which the new emperor and his son had delivered them. Among the spectators that day there were doubtless many Christians, who thus beheld the spectacle of Israel's ruin. But the sight would have given them other thoughts than those that moved their pagan neighbors. This evidence of Jewish sedition must have been a disturbing reminder of the fact that Jesus, the founder of their faith, had been executed for sedition against Rome. They would have seen that many of their fellow citizens were likely to view Christianity as Tacitus did when he wrote: "Christus, the founder of the name, had undergone the death penalty in the reign of Tiberius, by

sentence of the procurator Pontius Pilate, and the pernicious superstition was checked for a moment, only to break out once more, not merely in Judaea, the home of the disease, but in the capital itself . . ."

The Gospel of Mark reflects the position of the Roman Christians at this time with an amazing fidelity. There is one passage that, alone, unmistakably indicates the time and purpose of the Gospel's composition. In chapter 12:13–17 Jesus is questioned about the duty of Jews to pay tribute to Rome. Since this matter could have had no spiritual significance for the Christians of Rome, we may reasonably ask why the author of the Gospel devoted space to it. The answer can only be that the subject was politically important to the Roman Christians. This conclusion in turn raises the obvious question, when could the Christians in Rome have been thus interested in the attitude of Jesus to the Jewish obligation to pay tribute? The answer is equally obvious: when the issue had been so disturbingly intruded upon the attention of the Roman Christians by the Flavian triumph in A.D. 71.

In this passage about the tribute money the Jewish leaders are depicted as trying to make Jesus compromise himself on a matter that was a burning issue for the Jewish nationalists—the nonpayment of tribute was one of the causes of the revolt in 66. The author of the

7

Markan Gospel represents Jesus as endorsing the Jewish obligation to pay tribute to Caesar, but there are grounds for grave doubt that this was really the view of Jesus. The Markan presentation, however, was needed in Rome at this time, for it assured the Christians there, and any others who might read the Gospel, that Jesus was loyal to Rome and opposed to Jewish nationalism.

I have discussed the origins of the Gospel of Mark at length in order to evaluate its account of the trial of Jesus. On investigation this Gospel is found to be an account of Jesus composed by a member of the Christian community in Rome to meet the needs of his fellow Christians, in danger and perplexity owing to the Jewish War and the publicity given to it by the Flavian triumph in Rome. The apologetic purpose is evident in many ways, but the essential point of concern for the author of the Gospel was the Roman execution of Jesus. Even though he represented Jesus as loyal to Rome over the tribute question, there remained the undeniable fact that Pontius Pilate had crucified Jesus as a rebel. How was this awkward and disturbing fact to be explained?

The author of Mark endeavors to meet the difficulty by transferring the responsibility for the Crucifixion from the Roman governor to the Jewish leaders. He prepares for this by showing that the Jewish leaders, variously described as "the scribes and Pharisees" and the "high priests," had planned to destroy Jesus from the very start of his ministry. Thus we are told that after Jesus had healed a man with a withered hand on the Sabbath, "The Pharisees went out, and immediately held counsel with the Herodians against him, how to destroy him." The theme of the malicious intent of the Jewish authorities is gradually developed as the narrative proceeds. How this intent would be implemented is foretold in detail in a prophecy assigned to Jesus himself: "Behold, we are going up to Jerusalem; and the Son of Man will be delivered to the chief priests and the scribes, and they will condemn him to death, and deliver him to the Gentiles; and they will mock him, and spit upon him, and scourge him, and kill him; and after three days he will rise."

After describing further encounters with Jesus during the last days in Jerusalem, the Gospel of Mark relates how the Jewish leaders finally succeeded in arresting him, owing to the defection of one of his disciples. The fact is significant, for it indicates that Jesus was too strongly supported by the crowd for the Jewish authorities to arrest him publicly. The author of Mark does not say specifically why they then seized Jesus; we have only his earlier, general assertions that they had determined to destroy him from the beginning of his ministry.

The author of Mark admits that the Jewish authorities sent a heavily armed band to arrest Jesus, and that there was some armed resistance to his arrest in Gethsemane. He minimizes this resistance, saying, "one of those who

stood by drew his sword, and struck the slave of the high priest, and cut off his ear." He does not disclose, as the later Evangelists do, that the disciples were armed and that it was one of them who struck the blow.

After his arrest, according to the Gospel, Jesus was taken (it still apparently being night) before the Sanhedrin, the highest Jewish tribunal. The trial that followed is described in a way that raises a host of problems, both with regard to procedure and to what really happened. Mark's opening statement reiterates the theme of the evil intent of the Jewish leaders: "Now the chief priests and the whole council sought testimony against Jesus to put him to death; but they found none. For many bore false witness against him, and their witness did not agree." The impression that Mark's statements are evidently meant to convey is that the Jewish authorities, determined on destroying Jesus, used the trial as a legal pretext for accomplishing their aim. What is said about the "false witnesses," however, indicates a rather different situation. If they had suborned persons to give false evidence about Jesus, the Jewish leaders were strangely punctilious in rejecting that evidence when it was not mutually corroborated—surely they would have arranged things better, or been less scrupulous about the rules of evidence, if they had "rigged" the trial.

But the author of Mark was obviously more concerned

Jesus is denounced before Pilate by Annas and Caiaphas, the two high priests, in this painting from the Rossano manuscript.

with establishing the responsibility of the Jewish leaders for the Crucifixion than with presenting a logically coherent narrative. This also seems to explain his next statement. According to him, the only specific charge against Jesus was made when some "stood up and bore false witness against him, saying, 'We heard him say, "I will destroy this Temple that is made with hands, and in three days I will build another, not made with hands."' Yet not even so did their testimony agree." Mark describes this charge as "false witness," thereby suggesting that it was not true; and this suggestion is confirmed by the statement that the evidence of these witnesses did not agree. However, as John 2:19 and the Acts of the Apostles 6:14 indicate, there seems to have been a tradition in the primitive Christian community in Judaea that Jesus had made some utterance against the Temple; and Mark himself seems to imply this in 13:1–2.

Certain suggestions can be offered to elucidate the problem. In the first place it is unlikely that Jesus had actually threatened to destroy the Temple, for we know that his disciples continued to worship there and regarded it as the dwelling place of God; this devotion would be hard to explain if Jesus had so spoken against the Temple. Further, the accusation is rejected by Mark as false testimony. What seems the most probable solution is that the charge at the Sanhedrin trial arose out of the attack that Jesus had made a few days before on the Temple trading system. This system was necessary for the efficient running of the Temple cultus. Jews making the prescribed money offerings to the Temple had to change the Roman currency, with its graven images that were offensive to the sacred Law, into a suitable Temple currency. Those who came to offer sacrifices needed to buy sacrificial animals there. These facilities were licensed by the high priest. Such transactions, as well as the banking facilities offered by the Temple, provided a lucrative income to the sacerdotal aristocracy who managed the Temple. This aristocracy, moreover, controlled "native affairs" under the Romans: the high priest was appointed by the procurator. This pro-Roman aristocracy naturally was hated by patriotic Jews, and in attacking their trading organization in the Temple, Jesus was in effect attacking their control over the people and religion of Israel. There can be little doubt that Jesus' action in the Temple was a much more serious affair than it is represented to have been by Mark and the other Evangelists. And there is every reason to believe that it would have constituted one of the chief charges preferred against him. The Jewish authorities undoubtedly were concerned to discover what exactly was Jesus' intention in making this attack. Mark's curious reporting of the charge and of the conflict of evidence suggests that the Jewish authorities were unable to get a clear statement of what Jesus had said about his aims during his action in the Temple.

According to the Markan account of the Sanhedrin trial, after failing to get sufficient evidence about the Temple affair the high priest then asked Jesus directly whether he claimed to be the Messiah of Israel: "Are you the Christ [i.e., Messiah], the Son of the Blessed?" That he should have asked such a question, following on the Temple charge, clearly shows that the high priest connected revolutionary action with Messianic claims. In contemporary Jewish belief the Messiah would bring the existing world order to an end.

Mark reports Jesus as affirming that he *was* the Messiah, and the affirmation is stated in terms of current apocalyptic expectation: "I am; and you will see the Son of Man sitting on the right hand of Power, and coming with the clouds of heaven." The high priest takes this answer as a blasphemy, and, with the concurrence of the Sanhedrin, condemns Jesus to death.

Now we encounter one of the greatest problems of the Markan account. In the first place, although Josephus tells of many Messianic pretenders during the period A.D. 6–70, there is no record of any being condemned to death by the Sanhedrin for making such a claim. Secondly, according to Jewish Law the penalty for blasphemy was death by stoning—the death of Stephen provides a contemporary instance of this. But the Sanhedrin does not proceed to arrange for the execution of this sentence in the case of Jesus. Instead Mark goes on to relate, without a word of explanation, that in the morning the Jewish authorities handed Jesus over to Pontius Pilate. The charge preferred by them is not mentioned, but it was obviously a political one, for Pilate immediately asks Jesus, "Are you the King of the Jews?"

This action of the Jewish leaders, and the alteration of the charge, have caused much debate among scholars. There seems to be evidence that at this time the Sanhedrin could condemn on a capital charge, but the sentence had to be confirmed by the Roman governor. Presumably, if the Sanhedrin had condemned Jesus to death for blasphemy, they would have applied to Pilate for confirmation. If this had been given, Jesus would have been executed by stoning. That this was not so, and that Jesus was delivered to Pilate on a charge of sedition, indicates that the Jewish authorities were concerned with the political, not the religious, significance of Jesus. This concern is understandable. The high priest and the Sanhedrin were responsible to the Roman governor for Jewish affairs. Jesus' triumphal entry into Jerusalem and his action in the Temple had clearly disturbed the peace and good order of the Jewish state, besides challenging their own positions. That the Romans would hold them responsible for the continuance of the menace which Jesus constituted is attested by John 11:47–48, where Caiaphas, the high priest, is reported as saying to the Sanhedrin: "What are we to do? For this man performs many signs. If we let him go on thus, every one will believe in him, and the Romans will come and destroy both our holy place and our nation."

Consequently, the action taken by the Jewish leaders was in accordance with their responsibilities, and it anticipated Roman action. Having arrested Jesus, they examined him concerning his aims and supporters, preparatory to handing him over to Pilate. The charge was essentially a political one, although it must be remembered that politics and religion were inextricably bound together in Judaea at this time. The Gospel of Luke gives the most explicit account of the charges preferred against Jesus by the Jewish leaders: "We found this man perverting our nation, and forbidding us to give tribute to Caesar, and saying that he himself is Christ a king."

We must return to the Markan account, remembering that it is the earliest version. Mark represents Pilate as convinced of Jesus' innocence, "for he perceived that it was out of envy that the chief priests had delivered him up." Now, if this was indeed the opinion of Pilate, the course open to him was obvious. He had the authority and power to dismiss the case. We know a great deal about the character of Pilate from Philo of Alexandria and from Josephus, and they both describe Pilate as a tough-minded man, ready to use force, and not one to be intimidated by the Jewish leaders and people. Conse-

quently, if he had been convinced that Jesus was innocent, he was unlikely to have hesitated about thwarting the intention of the Jewish leaders. What Mark tells of his subsequent conduct at the trial is therefore difficult to reconcile with his character, as well as with logic.

Instead of dismissing the case, Pilate is depicted as trying to save Jesus by availing himself of an otherwise unknown custom. According to Mark, it was traditional at the Passover for the Roman governor to release a prisoner chosen by the crowd. There is no other evidence for such a custom, even in Josephus, who was careful to record all the privileges granted to the Jews by the Romans. But that is not all. Such a custom is inherently impossible. Judaea was seething with revolt; its government would have been annually frustrated by having to release a notable prisoner. According to Mark, on this occasion a dangerous rebel, probably a Zealot, was freed.

Even if we pass over the improbability of the existence of such a custom, what Mark tells of Pilate's use of it goes beyond belief. He depicts the tough Roman procurator, who was backed by a strong military force, as resorting to this custom to save a man he adjudged innocent and inviting the Jerusalem mob to choose between Jesus and a rebel leader, Barabbas, who had killed Romans in a recent insurrection. To have given the crowd such a choice would have been the height of folly if Pilate had really sought to save Jesus. The mob's decision was a foregone conclusion. Led by the chief priests, they naturally chose Barabbas, to them a patriotic hero. Frustrated, Pilate is represented as weakly asking the mob: "What shall I do with the man whom you call the King of the Jews?"

The picture of a Roman governor consulting a Jewish mob about what he should do with an innocent man is ludicrous in the extreme. But to this extreme the author of the Markan Gospel was evidently prepared to go, to explain away the problem of the Roman execution of Jesus. Thus he completes his picture of Jewish responsibility for the Crucifixion. The Jewish leaders, who were determined to destroy Jesus from the very beginning of his ministry, finally succeed in their fell design by forcing the reluctant Pilate to do their will. To round off this presentation of Jewish guilt, Mark describes the Jewish leaders, on Golgotha, as mocking the dying Jesus, while the Roman centurion recognizes his divinity as he dies: "Truly this man was the Son of God!" The death of Jesus is marked by the rending of the Temple Veil, thus symbolizing the obsolescence of the Jewish religion.

Mark's account of the career of Jesus and the circumstances of his Crucifixion would have been welcomed by

Pilate offers to free either Jesus or Barabbas, who stands in chains at lower right in this Rossano Gospel miniature. On Pilate's left a group of Jews call for the crucifixion of Jesus.

ϨϢΝΔϵΠΙΛΑΤΟϹΟΤΙϵΚΤΗϹϵΞΟΥϹΙΑϹΗΡΩΔΟΥϵϹΤΙΝΑΝϵΠϵΜΨϵΝΑ
ϵΝΡΩϢΔΗΝΟΝΤΑΚΑΙΑΥΤΟΝϵΝΙϵΡΟϹΟΛΥΜΟΙϹϵΝΤΑΥΤΙϹΤΑΙϹΗΜϵΡ

ΒΑΡΑΒ
ΒΔϹ

the Christians of Rome. The embarrassment of Jesus' execution for sedition against Rome was alleviated by placing the responsibility on the Jews. Far from condemning Jesus to death, the Roman Christians now knew that Pilate actually recognized his innocence and tried to save him. Moreover, Jesus had given proof of his loyalty to Rome in the matter of the tribute, and the Roman centurion had been the first to perceive his divinity. The Jewish leaders who had plotted his death, and the Jewish people who had demanded it, had

brought upon their nation the catastrophe of A.D. 70.

Mark's explanation of the Roman execution of Jesus, motivated as it had been by the needs of the Christian community in Rome in A.D. 71, exercised a formative influence on subsequent Christian tradition. The writers of the Gospels of Matthew and Luke accepted it, elaborating upon it according to the particular requirements of the communities for which they wrote. Their additions were inspired by the need to allay a belief widespread in the Roman Empire that Christianity was

ALINARI

The great triumph celebrating the conquest of Jerusalem is vividly depicted on the Arch of Titus in Rome. In the detail to the left, the Temple booty is paraded through the streets.

Jesus here, had a poignant significance in the light of the disaster that had befallen the Palestinian Jews as a result of their resort to war.

Another addition that Matthew makes to the Markan account of the trial of Jesus was destined to have tragic consequences for the Jewish people. To emphasize the innocence of Jesus, Pilate is shown as publicly repudiating responsibility for the condemnation of Jesus. He symbolically washes his hands before the people, declaring, "I am innocent of this man's blood." The Jewish people are made to answer: "His blood be on us and on our children!" The legacy of these words has been terrible; they have been cited to justify centuries of Christian persecution of the Jews. It is significant that only at the recent Vatican Council has a formal declaration been made exonerating subsequent generations of Jews from responsibility for the murder of Christ.

The historian who seeks to understand why the Romans executed Jesus for sedition has first to investigate the Gospel of Mark, as we have endeavored to do here. He has to penetrate Mark's apologetic presentation to discern what really happened on that first Good Friday. So far as a reasonable assessment can be made, it would seem that the Jewish authorities arrested Jesus because they regarded him as a menace to the peace and well-being of the Jewish state, for which they were responsible to the Romans. After interrogating Jesus, they handed him over to Pontius Pilate, accusing him of seditious teaching and action. Pilate, who probably knew something of Jesus' activities, accepted the charge and commanded his crucifixion. He gave orders that the *titulus*, an inscription placed at the head of the cross stating the reason for a criminal's condemnation, should read: "This is Jesus, the King of the Jews." Pilate also ordered that two *lestai* should be crucified with Jesus. The fact is significant, for we know that the Romans called the Zealots, the Jewish resistance fighters, *lestai*, i.e., brigands. These men had doubtless taken part in the recent insurrection in Jerusalem. That Jesus was crucified between two rebels surely indicates that Pilate regarded him as such.

Thus, to the extent that the historian can today evaluate the evidence concerning the Roman execution of Jesus, it would seem that Pontius Pilate regarded Jesus as guilty of sedition. Whether he was right in his assessment is another matter.

S. G. F. Brandon, who teaches at Manchester University in England, is the author of the book Jesus and the Zealots. *This article is adapted from an essay that originally appeared in the English publication* History Today.

in origin and nature a revolutionary movement. Thus the Gospel of Matthew expands Mark's brief and reticent mention of the armed resistance in Gethsemane by representing Jesus as rebuking the disciple who drew the sword: "Put your sword back into its place; for all who take the sword will perish by the sword." The author of this Gospel was writing for a Jewish Christian community, probably in Alexandria, where there was a great need to damp down revolutionary feeling after the fall of Jerusalem in A.D. 70. The words, attributed to

By PAUL BROOKS

The Rhinoceros at Bay

He may not be, at first glance, the most lovable of beasts, but those who know him feel that his threatened extinction would be an irreparable loss

O f all creatures on earth, the rhinoceros appears at first glance the least likely to be associated with the art of love. The great horn that decorates his nose, and from which his name is derived, is not generally considered an object of beauty or endearment. Yet the belief in this horn's aphrodisiac and other magical properties has existed for countless centuries. And incredible as the fact may seem, the persistence of this belief down to our own day is a deadly threat to the existence of the comparatively few rhinos left on earth. Their battle for survival involves elements as dramatic and bizarre as any that can be found in the annals of conservation.

In the story of the rhino one can see a head-on collision of modern science and ancient myth. For instance, many

otherwise rational persons still think in terms of "good animals" and "bad animals"; they cherish the dove and the deer, they hate the hawk and the wolf. With that "living fossil," the rhinoceros, the situation is more complicated. He is neither loved nor hated, but he has been senselessly persecuted and misunderstood. Few people know, or care, about his present predicament. They scarcely even realize that he comes in various shapes and sizes, some of which may soon be permanently off the market.

Why should they care? For one reason, because the rhino, more than any other great mammal, is a living link between our world and the world of the past. Of the many types of rhinoceros that once walked the earth—including the woolly rhino that was a

contemporary of the mammoth—five species have lasted until today: two in Africa and three in Asia. All five can be traced far back into the Tertiary period, before the Ice Age, long before the emergence of man.

When we think of rhinos, the picture that flashes on the mind's eye is almost always that of the black rhinoceros of the African bush (*Diceros bicornis*)—prize subject for every photographic safari (anyone can get a chilling shot of a rhino's "charge" from the safety of a moving Land-Rover) and, in African wildlife films, the short-sighted old curmudgeon who provides artistic contrast to the light-footed, frolicking gazelles. Far less known is the African square-lipped or white rhinoceros (*Ceratotherium simum*), recently rescued from the verge

The formidable bulk of the black rhinoceros (opposite) hardly suggests the delicate unicorn (above), yet the latter slipped into mythology as a metamorphosis of the rhino.

15

of extinction. And few people indeed have seen all three of the Asian species: the Great Indian or one-horned rhinoceros (*Rhinoceros unicornis*), now surviving precariously in Nepal, Bengal, and Assam in northeast India; the Javan (*Rhinoceros sondaicus*) and the Sumatran (*Didermocerus sumatrensis*), both of which have all but disappeared.

To understand the rhinos' situation today, to take practical means that they shall not perish—leaving this earth so much the poorer—we must turn back upstream to the days of Marco Polo and Europe's first contact with Cathay. It is a tortuous voyage, full of crosscurrents and dark whirlpools where myth and science join and separate and join again. The object of the search is the most treasured animal of the medieval world; the most treasured and necessarily the most elusive, since its value depended on the fact that it did not exist.

The unicorn that faces the lion on the British coat of arms, or the delicate prancing creature of The Unicorn Tapestries (see pages 15 and 21), seems about as remote from a rhinoceros as a butterfly from a caterpillar—and is as close. At the base of the unicorn legend, as Odell Shepard showed in his *Lore of the Unicorn*, lay distorted descriptions of the rhinoceros, whose features were blended with those of other animals such as that long-horned antelope, the oryx. Aelian, a third-century Roman writer, repeats from hearsay that "there are mountains in the interior of India which are inaccessible to men and therefore full of wild beasts. Among these is the unicorn"—and goes on to describe an animal which has the mane of a horse, the feet of an elephant, and the tail of a goat, with "a single black horn between its brows," an animal of "great strength of body" and solitary habits. A strange compound, but obviously more rhinoceros than anything else. By the Middle Ages the connection between rhinoceros and unicorn is taken for granted. Describing Lesser Java (now Sumatra), one of the remote kingdoms of the great Khan, Marco Polo writes:

"They have wild elephants and plenty of unicorns, which are scarcely smaller than elephants. They have the hair of a buffalo and feet like an elephant's. They have a single large, black horn in the middle of the forehead . . . They have a head like a wild boar's and always carry it stooped toward the ground. They spend their time by preference wallowing in mud and slime. They are very ugly brutes to look at. They are not at all such as we describe them when we relate that they let themselves be captured by virgins, but clean contrary to our notions." This is a composite picture of the one-horned Javan and Sumatran rhinoceros, the latter of which in youth at least is somewhat hairy. The business of capture by virgins—who do not seem per se the ideal choice for such rough work—is baffling unless one is familiar with the approved method of hunting the unicorn. The technique is described in Richard de Fournival's *Bestiare d'amour:* "For this is the nature of the unicorn, that no other beast is so hard to capture, and he has one horn on his nose which no armor can withstand, so that no one dares go forth against him except a virgin girl . . . Therefore wise huntsmen who know his nature set a virgin in his way; he falls asleep in her lap; and while he sleeps the hunters, who would not dare approach him when awake, come up and kill him." An unsportsmanlike procedure, but in a field where anything is fair. For we are dealing here less with the chase than with that other blood sport, the art of love.

The valuable part of the unicorn was, of course, the horn. In days when poisoning was an accepted method of political advancement, the well-known fact that a unicorn horn would sweat or change color in the presence of poison made it a useful adjunct to the banquet table. Up to the sixteenth century physicians prescribed powdered unicorn horn "as a cure for all poisons, for fevers, for bites of mad dogs and scorpions, for falling sickness, worms, fluxes, loss of memory, the plague, and [to bring about] prolongation of

youth." Most of these uses are now obsolete. It is the "prolongation of youth" that persists. One has only to substitute the rhino's horn for the unicorn's to realize the ancient origins of our present conservation problem. The medical evidence that rhino horn has no effect on people—except perhaps a psychological one—is blissfully disregarded, or unknown, by today's purchasers.

Unicorn horns, or "alicorns," were kings' treasures. Benvenuto Cellini tells of one that Pope Clement VII presented to Francis I of France in honor of the marriage of the pope's niece, Catherine de Médicis, to Francis's son. Up to the time of their Civil War, the English treasured the "Horn of Windsor," which once belonged to Queen Elizabeth I. According to Hakluyt, this fine horn was picked up on an island in Frobisher's Strait in the Arctic. The story rings true, since the alicorn of medieval Europe—the straight, sharp, spiral horn depicted in The Unicorn Tapestries—was in actuality the single spearlike tusk of that Arctic member of the whale family, the narwhal. The equally real, if less beautiful, horn of the rhino entered Europe from the opposite direction, through the growing trade with the Indies. Like alicorns, rhino horns were carved into drinking cups to safeguard against poison, as they still are in Nepal and parts of India. In the form of a powder, rhino horn was also used as an antidote for all ills, including impotence. Eventually, however, with the

The Indian rhinoceroses at left are protected from poachers in a wildlife sanctuary at Kaziranga; unprotected ones often come to an ignoble end in a shop window—as in Yokohama, opposite, where whole and shredded rhino horn are both displayed for sale as presumed aphrodisiacs.

coming of the age of reason and the advent of modern medicine, the bottom fell out of the market for rhino horn in the Western world. In the East, on the contrary, it is literally worth its weight in gold.

As a creation of man's imagination, the unicorn is immortal. His living prototype, however, may be doomed to disappear through man's agency, after existing for millions of years. The rhino has become a symbol of an almost lost world. Fearful of aspect, solitary by nature, he precariously holds his own in parts of Africa and Asia—the two continents on which the great beasts of the past have not wholly succumbed to advancing civilization. Making his acquaintance, however casually, has its special rewards. As we look back at the recent history of the two African and the three Asian rhinos, we become aware of how many facets there are to the complex problem of wildlife conservation.

To those who have lived and worked with rhinos I apologize in advance for the occasional use of the first person. Even the most fleeting experience has more life than a statistic. Some would argue, of course, that a biographer should never meet his subject at all, lest he be seduced by the latter's charm. Here I plead guilty from the start.

The first rhinoceros I ever met outside a zoo was seven months old, no larger than a medium-sized pig, and utterly charming. He was a black

African rhino and belonged to Nick Carter, a former game warden then living at Kiboko (Swahili for "hippopotomus") in Kenya. Kiboko is a sort of oasis on the long dry road from Nairobi to Mombasa, the home of the late J. A. Hunter, one of the last of the old-time white hunters and a ruthless slaughterer of rhinos. The baby, named Little Owl, had been adopted by Nick when his mother was killed by poachers. Though for obvious reasons he was not given the run of the house, he achieved the same end by pushing down, like a miniature bulldozer, any barrier that was put in his way. He could not bear to have Nick, his adopted "mother," out of his sight. Toward guests he was as friendly as a puppy, but more dignified.

Back of the house were three heavy stockades. One was empty; the other two each contained a full-grown wild rhino: a male and a pregnant female. Nick's extraordinary task, which had made him known throughout East Africa, was to transfer the remaining animals from unprotected areas such as the Kiboko region, where they were being poached for the sake of their horns, to the safety of the national parks. Through great courage and persistence, aided by a trained staff of native game scouts, he had perfected a unique method of hunting rhinos. His weapon was a homemade crossbow shooting darts loaded with anesthetic. A dart in the rump would knock the beast out for a brief period, during which it was bound, loaded on a truck

by means of winch and rollers, and transferred to one of the stockades. There it was examined and treated for any injuries or disease, after which it was transported by truck to a national park and released. In summary it sounds simple. It wasn't.

I never saw Nick capture a rhino, though we had one good morning's hunt. We were up at six. Half the party rode in a Land-Rover whose front fender had been crumpled by a beleaguered rhino some weeks earlier. The other half rode in the truck, looking, in Nick's words, "like aristocrats in a tumbril." Crash helmets were *de rigueur* for everyone. As the Land-Rover turned off the "track" into the bush, I could see why. It was rough country, mostly grassland and scattered scrub, thickets of thorn trees, and an occasional huge baobab standing in grotesque splendor. The place was full of wildlife. Flocks of yellow-legged francolin flushed ahead of us, red-billed hornbills flapped heavily by, wart hogs with flaglike tails erect paraded into the bush, and a herd of zebras galloped parallel to our course, raising a red dust against the rising sun. As we approached a shy, solitary oryx, I was reminded of the unicorn. One can well understand how his spearlike horns, seen at a distance by a credulous observer, might be taken for a single horn springing from the forehead. The Arabian oryx, which once ranged through much of the Near East, is doubtless a secondary source of the unicorn legend. Indeed, his

17

A unicorn is about to lay his head in a maiden's lap, signifying purity, in this French tapestry dating from about 1600. The lion, who also faces a unicorn on the British Royal Arms, here symbolizes ancient lineage and power. Modern rather than medieval concepts of maidenly purity are reflected in the contemporary print opposite, made by John Wesley, entitled Dream of Unicorns.

graceful body is much closer to representations of that mythical creature than the great hulk of the rhinoceros, and his lovely head is a far likelier burden for a maiden's lap.

Bouncing through the bush, we found fresh rhino signs, but no rhino. We did find a Volkswagen, belonging to poachers, cleverly concealed in the underbrush. (Our Kikuyu hunters deflated the tires and removed the distributor, hoping to cause some embarrassment when the next quick getaway was in order.) Farther along, a lioness leapt across our bows. Then a Very light went up from the truck, by now a mile or more away. They had sighted a rhino. After a brief exchange on the walkie-talkie, we raced to join them. When we arrived, the beast had disappeared, but his tracks were easy to follow in the light ash of a burned-over stretch of grassland. Two Kikuyu trackers, keen and graceful as bird dogs, jogged ahead of

the Land-Rover. Then abruptly the burned area ended and the tracks faded away into concealing grass. We kept on hopefully and once, at the glimpse of a dark shape, Nick readied his crossbow. But it turned out to be an ostrich. By now the sun was high, and we reluctantly headed back to Kiboko, our disappointment lightened by the sight of a whole herd of oryx and, as we approached the river, a group of statuesque waterbuck. Nick would catch up with the rhino another day.

Though concerned specifically with the black rhinoceros, Nick Carter's operation involved important principles and techniques applicable to other threatened species. Specimens of the rare Hunter's antelope, for example, have been captured in Kenya's Northern Frontier District, where political turmoil makes protection all but impossible, and released in the game parks of the south. Most spectacular was a recent project to save the

Arabian oryx. Ruthless hunting with jeeps and tommy guns had reduced this beautiful animal from its former abundance to about two hundred individuals scattered through the desert. A team of experts successfully pursued and roped three of them, and flew them to Phoenix, Arizona. In a large enclosure, together with several individuals contributed by zoos, they have thrived and bred. The only disturbing factor is that, for some unknown reason, the first nine offspring have all been males.

As late as 1900 the black rhino was to be found throughout all of Africa south of the Sahara, excluding only the rain forests of West Africa and the Congo. A traveler wrote at the turn of the century: "From all sportsmen and prospectors who have visited out-of-the-way districts I have heard the same story of the great number of these fine old beasts." The rhino's

tough hide was a protection against primitive native weapons, but not against the modern high-powered rifle. He was killed off as a nuisance in the neighborhood of settlements, and he was slaughtered in the name of sport. The trade in horns was staggering. Today the rhino's only chance for survival is national parks and wildlife reserves. The disappearance of the rhino may be a major factor in the deterioration of the habitat itself: by feeding on coarse and prickly vegetation, rhinos have probably helped to maintain the equilibrium between bush and open grassland, in semi-arid areas. Now the balance is being upset. Such are the interconnections in the seamless web of life.

The web of superstition is almost as far-reaching and complex. Shift the scene to a hole-in-the-wall druggist's shop in Taipei, capital of Taiwan. There, in December, 1965, I saw the sordid last act of a tragedy that had

begun with death somewhere in the African bush. In the shop's showcase was a weird assortment of supposed aphrodisiacs. There was ginseng root, which the Chinese have accepted as a substitute for the vanishing mandrake ("Go, and catch a falling star/Get with child a mandrake root"). There were antlers and dried sexual organs of a deer. And in the center display case was the unmistakable horn of an African black rhino, for sale at seventy-five dollars an ounce. Though scientific analysis of the horn has shown that its ingestion cannot, except in the imagination, have any rejuvenating effect, this is of little concern to the dealer who makes an enormous profit on the sale, or to the poacher who kills the animal. Unfortunately the rhino, of all animals, is most vulnerable to poaching pressures. Like the elephant, it has a low rate of reproduction; only the longevity of the individual enables the species to survive. And so long as

the myth of the horn's magic power persists throughout much of the Far East, only strict policing can save it.

The history of the other African species, the white or square-lipped rhinoceros, is parallel to that of the black rhino, though in some ways it is both more shocking and more encouraging. The "white" rhino, incidentally, is gray, not white. Its name comes from *weit*, Afrikaans for "wide," and refers to its great square muzzle; it is a grazer, not a browser. Scientifically it is divided into two subspecies: an isolated northern population in Uganda and the Sudan (well known to the ancient world) and the more familiar, and once so abundant, subspecies of the south.

Almost as heavy as a hippopotamus, the white rhino is twice the size of the black but much gentler. Indeed, one naturalist who knows the species well finds that on close acquaintance it

19

"seems so helpless and confused that one feels inclined to comfort this huge pachyderm." This approachability, together with its habit (unique among the rhino tribe) of grazing in groups in open grassland, made the white rhino peculiarly vulnerable. To the well-armed hunter it was easy game, and profitable. It was taken not only for its horn but for its hide—which was prized for making whips—and for its tasty flesh. As a result the white rhino was virtually wiped out.

First described by early nineteenth-century travelers, the southern race of the white rhino was then to be found throughout South Africa. Its decline began with the coming of firearms in the hands of European hunters. As late as 1871 it was reported still numerous in uninhabited parts of the Transvaal, in southern Rhodesia, and in the southern part of Mozambique. About that time wholesale slaughter began. Two white hunters, for example, recorded killing eighty rhinos in a single season. A European trader in southern Rhodesia, employing some four hundred native hunters, all but exterminated the rhinos in his territory. By the 1890's the species was considered practically extinct; as with the American bison, only bleached skulls remained to indicate its former range. Then in 1897, just before it would have disappeared forever from the earth, two game reserves were established in Natal, and a few white rhinos given refuge in them. In 1920 the estimated number of white rhinos was twenty. By 1929 it was a hundred and twenty; by 1932, two hundred and twenty; and by 1959, six hundred. Today there are more animals than the two small reserves can support. In a spectacular program of live transportation, using the drug technique, white rhinos are being shipped to game reserves throughout Africa, as well as to zoos in other parts of the world. Kruger Park received ninety of them in 1964. During the same year, in a reserve in the Transvaal, occurred a momentous birth: the first white rhino to be born outside Natal in seventy years!

We speak of a "brush with death"; here is a "brush with extinction" to make the conservationist shudder, but also to give him heart. It shows that no situation is entirely hopeless when modern scientific knowledge and strict enforcement of the law are brought into play.

The rescue of the African white rhino is an example of what can be done when we care enough to do it. Preservation of African wildlife has, in recent years, become a world-wide concern. But what of Asia, the other continent that still harbors remnants of the world's great tropical fauna? Short of a miracle, two of the three Asian species of rhinoceros seem doomed. The Sumatran, smallest of living rhinos, was formerly found throughout southeast Asia. As late as the 1920's it was abundant in the Mekong valley, and hunted in the vicinity of Saigon. Today the few remaining animals are scattered from Burma to Sumatra. Since they are mostly in rugged mountain country and thick forest far from human settlement, no one really knows how many have survived. Part of the rhino's favorite habitat has become a battlefield; but even where war does not pursue him, poachers do. When a rhino is sighted, it is generally tracked to its death. There are well-attested stories of one Chinese trader in Sumatra who had a standing order of twenty-five hundred dollars for a large horn, and of another who was offering a new American car for a whole carcass—since the blood and various organs are also considered medicinal.

The Javan rhinoceros, a close relative of the Great Indian, is gone from its once extensive range on the mainland. An estimated two to four dozen individuals maintain a precarious existence in the Udjung Kulon Reserve, a peninsula at the westernmost tip of Java. The exploding human population, with its need for agricultural land, has all but squeezed them out. That they exist at all is probably due to an incident unique in the annals of conservation, which is not without its grim humor. Immediately after the

last war, when the Japanese guards for the reserve had been withdrawn and not yet replaced by the local government, a notorious Chinese poacher entered the reserve to kill the last of the rhinos for their horns. However, he was promptly killed himself by a still rarer animal, the Javan tiger. Thus other poachers were frightened off. One vanishing species had unwittingly saved the other.

"I went . . . to see the rhinoceros, or unicorn," wrote John Evelyn in his diary for October 22, 1684, "being the first I suppose was ever brought to England." It was a Great Indian rhinoceros—the only Asian species most of us can hope to see today. A live rhino had appeared in western Europe almost two centuries earlier, shipped from Goa, on the western coast of India, around the Horn to Lisbon; and some years later another was sent as a present to the king of Portugal. A sketch of this animal—plus a large dose of artistic imagination—is said to be the source for Albrecht Dürer's well-known engraving (see page 116).

In those days the rhino flourished over a large part of northern India as far west as the coast and north to Kashmir. But as wilderness gave way to cultivation, the Indian rhino's lebensraum shrank to a few pinpoints on the map. An estimated six hundred animals survive, most of them in sanctuaries in Nepal and in the Kaziranga Wildlife Sanctuary in Assam, which I was able to visit last winter.

Has any park in the world such a dramatic approach? From Calcutta your plane flies due north—to avoid East Pakistan—toward Mt. Kanchenjunga, its snow-covered massif dazzling-white in the early morning sun. Westward rises the summit of Everest. A right-angle turn, and the course lies along the broad Brahmaputra valley. Everywhere the brown earth is under cultivation, in rice paddies or tea gardens stretching to the horizon. Then directly below appears a green oasis of tall grass and swamp and luxuriant forest cover. This is Kaziranga. Some twenty-five miles long and eight miles

CONTINUED ON PAGE 116

A well-known tapestry made for the French court depicts the capture of a unicorn near the royal palace

GREAT ARTISTS AND THEIR WORLDS

BRUEGEL

Through his rollicking pictures of peasant life

shines a sober philosophy of man's place in nature

By JOHN CANADAY

Even more extremely than most great painters, Pieter Bruegel the Elder exists at two levels. At the popular one, his fantastic drolleries and his pictures of rollicking peasants are taken at face value and bought by the thousands in reproduction. At this level Bruegel is certainly as curious and delightful a painter as you could find—but only curious and delightful. At his true level, when these obvious charms are recognized as nothing but a pictorial skin, Bruegel is discoverable as an extraordinarily complex painter-philosopher. He stands with the small company of the greatest artists of any time and place, and in his own century he was the only genius to appear in northern art between Dürer and Rubens.

Very little is known about his life, but when he died in 1569 he was probably not much beyond the age of forty and perhaps had not even reached it. He materializes for the first time in a document of 1551, when he was accepted as a master in the Antwerp painters' guild.

Assuming that he went through the usual mill of apprenticeship, he would have been in his early twenties, so that he was probably born between 1525 and 1530. Several Netherlandish towns claim honor as the locale.

With very few facts available to support wishful conclusions drawn from his art, it is possible but dangerous to reconstruct a personality called Pieter Bruegel. A good beginning is to reject a couple of imposters born of loose romanticizing between the nominal subjects of his paintings and the popular conviction that all artists must be a little freakish. First there is the picaresque adventurer Bruegel, who loved drinking and dancing with the peasants at their festivals, and then went home to record village weddings and harvest feasts in genre paintings. At the other extreme there is the Bruegel invented to explain his fantastic paintings, apparently the member of some secret religious cult whose esoteric and even diabolic catechism could be set down only dis-

The Peasant Dance (above) is anything but a scene of pure rustic jollity. In this section of Bruegel's painting, lust, anger, and gluttony mingle with joy and the excitement of a Netherlandish kermis, or church fair.

guised in cabalistic symbols or allegories.

Either of these Bruegels is as false as the other, both are simple-minded, and neither is supportable. Whatever else he was, the real Bruegel was a man whose interests in common people and in fantastic invention were neither discordant nor contradictory, but were interdependent aspects of reflections upon the nature of man, his relationship to himself and his small world, and to the cosmos that turns that world through its seasons.

That much we can see in the paintings, but all efforts to particularize this man are frustrated. Even his name is variously spelled and misspelled (as "Breughel"); he himself changed Brueghel to Bruegel about 1559, but the "h" was retained by several generations of his descendants. Certainly he was famous and successful, since the Habsburgs were among his patrons, with the result that the finest concentration of Bruegels is now in neither Antwerp nor Brussels (he worked in both cities) but in Vienna. He must have been well educated, since he was part of the liberal humanist circle that included Abraham Ortelius, Plantin, Frans Hogenberg, and Goltzius, and he was not there as court jester. The single fact we know about his personal life is that in 1653—when he would have been between thirty-three and thirty-eight, with six years to live—he made a respectable marriage to Mayken, the daughter of the painter Pieter Coecke van Aelst (who may have been his teacher). Their two sons, only babies when their father died, grew up to become prominent artists—as did three grandsons and five great-grandsons, all painters named Brueghel. (Of the long list, the two sons are the most important. The first, named for his father but nicknamed "Hell" because of his penchant for painting conflagrations, remains a moderately interesting artist in his rather washed-out continuation of the Bosch-Bruegel hellscape. The younger son, Jan, nicknamed "Velvet," is a really charming painter in his own right, parentage aside.)

Bruegel lived during a time of social, political, and religious upheaval that affected him directly, but his convictions are known only through deduction from his art. In the case of Dürer a little earlier, we can follow in his letters, in his writings, and in the recorded comments of his friends the moral agonies and aesthetic arguments that determined the nature of his art. But we have not one single helpful word from or about Bruegel in this respect; it is impossible to think of him as orthodox in politics or religion at a time when orthodoxy was so often tainted by bigotry or tyranny, but what deviations he admitted, what loyalties he held, we cannot know.

We must always come back to his paintings, and here at least we can discover three general principles of belief:

Men as individuals are faulty, and their most degrading sin is materialism, with covetousness and avarice as the most crippling symptoms of their folly.

But generically, man is noble, heroic. In a state close to nature (although Bruegel must not be thought of quite as a proto-Rousseauist) man comes closest to realizing this potential.

And the proof of man's dignity is that he is worthy of inclusion as an integral part of the rhythm of the cosmos, which identifies the tempo of man's life with the majestic succession of night and day and the turn of the seasons, which accepts him without question and without privilege as part of an ineffable complex that unifies everything from the flight of a bird to the circling of the planets.

Even in rudimentary summary, Bruegel's premises are quite obviously his answers to questions that men have always asked themselves. The concept of man as heroic but men as faulty has cousins everywhere. In ancient Greece it was the noble being with the tragic flaw, but in Bruegel the flaw is no longer tragic but contemptible, because remediable; no implacable fate declares that there is no way out. In the Book of Genesis innocence in Paradise is lost through original sin, but in Bruegel man need not suffer forever for having yielded to an appetite in a moment of weakness; he is free to enjoy his appetites so long as he has the strength not to abuse them, and he needs no Redeemer to restore him to bliss because he finds his own bliss in identification with the cosmos.

Bruegel's cosmos and its rhythm have an even more thickly branched family tree, spreading in one direction as far as India. Some of his own landscapes (as we shall see) were immediate continuations of a section of the theologically organized universe of the Middle Ages, in which every single thing and every single activity had its defined place. But the medieval universe was almost too neat, like a tremendous globular filing cabinet surrounded by a void; its minor virtue of tidiness imposed the major flaw of static definition. In Bruegel's universe nothing is static: everything moves, grows, and responds in endless harmonies of action and interaction.

Bruegel's scenes of peasant life are so rich in human detail that they repay the closest scrutiny. Above is the full painting from which a section has been reproduced on the preceding two pages. Opposite is a small detail of that detail.

Dulle Griet or "Mad Meg" (above), probably painted in 1562, displays the kind of fantastic invention that often appears in Bruegel's work alongside his sharp observation of peasant life. The detail opposite shows Meg herself striding through Hell.

Finally, in his more vigorous way, Bruegel anticipated intellectually the nineteenth-century romantics' emotional identification of man with nature, but without falling into the romantic fallacy of endowing nature with emotions corresponding to man's.

The only concept of the nature of things that seems never to have occurred to Bruegel is our objective scientific one by which the cosmos becomes something physically explicable and hence godless. As for Bruegel's God, we have already said that his religious affiliation can only be surmised, and the usual surmise is that he was a deviant Catholic. But when he painted Biblical subjects he painted them in his own terms, neither manufacturing them according to the formulas that enabled even the most unreligious painters to turn out satisfactory holy pictures nor giving them any Christian-mystical turn of his own.

The Massacre of the Innocents (page 28), beneath its nominal subject, is a *sub rosa* indictment of the devastation of the Netherlandish populace by Spanish military force. *The Procession to Calvary* becomes an execution scene concerned less with the victim than with exposing the baseness of human beings who can watch his suffer-

ings with callous indifference. *Christ and the Woman Taken in Adultery*, ostensibly a parable pleading for charitable compassion between human beings, is extended to a social allegory of religious intolerance. And *The Numbering at Bethlehem* is at first glance a genre scene, where the protagonists, Joseph and Mary, are all but lost in the crowd as they enter a snowy Netherlandish village where the census takers are busily at work in the midst of the villagers' daily life.

But *The Numbering at Bethlehem* also shows Mary joyously shielding with her cloak the glorious secret that she carries in her womb. Thus she becomes a symbol of the presence of miracle ignored in the petty bustle of everyday affairs. This is a subtheme in Bruegel's consummate expressions of his beliefs, the landscapes with figures that have no specifically religious subject. Just as the villagers are blind to the presence of a miracle in *The Numbering at Bethlehem*, so are the men who plod across the landscape of *The Hunters in the Snow* (pages 36–37) oblivious to anything but the business at hand. If we recognize their integration with the cosmic rhythm, *they* are too busy even to suspect it.

This "religion" of the cosmos was surely not some-

Though Biblical in subject, The Massacre of the Innocents, *1565–67, is set in a wintry Netherlandish locale. In the slaughter of Jewish infants by Herod's soldiers, Bruegel may have seen a parallel to the cruel occupation of the Netherlands by Spanish armies. The detail opposite shows a horseman of King Herod (or Philip II) riding down a Jewish (or Flemish) woman.*

thing that Bruegel thought of as religion. But a man's true religion is whatever he believes most deeply, and by this definition Bruegel was a pantheist. On the evidence of his paintings, his God was not a force that could be isolated as a central personality—was not the Biblical God who created the universe in the beginning and rules it forever—but an all-pervading force, the life force if you wish, that is manifested equally in every detail of a universe that is self-existing.

Fortunately Bruegel was in the habit of dating his paintings, and in chronological succession they show that he reached his conclusions, or at least expressed his beliefs, in the order we have listed—that man is faulty, that he is potentially noble, and that his existence is legitimized by his position as an integral but not central unit of the cosmos—although not within such arbitrarily neat compartments. The best way to pull these remarks together is to summarize Bruegel's development with a few examples of his paintings. But it is time just now to insert a reminder that no matter how profound or how complicated the philosophical aspects of his work may

be, the popular Bruegel shares with the other Bruegel one characteristic vital to both: a tremendous gusto, a full-blooded heartiness, an ebullient curiosity about the visual world and an irrepressible appreciation of its rich physical satisfactions. Even if he had had nothing else to offer, this gusto would set Bruegel off by himself with no rival except his fellow countryman Rubens, who in the next century responded as fully, in his more princely way, to the same stimuli.

In 1552, the year after his acceptance as master in the Antwerp guild, Bruegel made the Italian trip that for northern painters was becoming almost a required postgraduate apprenticeship. He must have left home with the standard list of things to see, and with introductions to Italian painters. But the drawings he brought back, the only testimony to the trip, indicate that his interests were altogether unconventional. The journey was unusually lengthy, since Bruegel got as far as Sicily, and if along the way he studied classical monuments and the Renaissance paintings that other artists went to see, his responses were not the usual ones.

Nature, not other men's art, was Bruegel's study on this trip, in all the dramatic variety that Italy offered in contrast to the intimate monotony of his native landscape. He crossed the Alps, and his drawings of mountains—great peaks and ranges seen from above by an artist who had never seen things from a perch higher than a housetop—are comparable only to Leonardo's, but they differ in a significant way: Leonardo's mountainscapes (or cosmoscapes) are generalized to recall the geological forces that created them; even the cities that appear here and there in Leonardo's valleys are presented as natural growths (which cities are) rather than accumulations of habitations; they seem unpopulated. Bruegel's mountainscapes are more detailed; their valleys are nooks and crannies sympathetic to human existence, places where men can fulfill their function as recognized parts of a world even so vast.

For the rest of his life, the view from above, even of a flat landscape or of an interior, became Bruegel's consistent vantage point. The fulfillment of his interest in landscape, however, had to wait. He seems to have returned to the Netherlands in 1554, was certainly back in Antwerp by 1555, and in 1556 suddenly began the fantasy-moralities that brought him the sobriquet "Pieter the Droll." "Droll" carried implications beyond the merely humorous, edging into the sinister and terrible, and in this field young Bruegel's mentor by example was Hieronymus Bosch—dead since 1516 but still the great master (as he remains today) of moral allegory in the form of diableries. Bruegel's professional mentor was Hieronymus Cock, an Antwerp print dealer who had commissioned him to do drawings for engravings on such salable subjects as the deadly sins.

Bruegel was known to the mass of his contemporaries only through these prints. As a painter he executed none of those public commissions, such as altarpieces or decorations for civic buildings, that were accessible to everybody. His patrons were diplomats, statesmen, and wealthy intellectuals—art collectors on an international scale, men like the Cardinal Antoine Perrenot de Granvella, Archbishop of Malines and adviser to Philip II of Spain, or the geographer and humanist Ortelius.

Nearly twenty-five years after Bruegel's death when the Archduke Ernst became Governor of the Nether-

Om dar dr werdt is sor ongaru
Dar on gba ir mdaru

Bruegel is at his most humane in
The Cripples (opposite), *painted
in 1568. These "poor stepchildren
of fate" are lepers. The Misanthrope* (right), *of the same year,
is inscribed "Because the world is
so faithless I am going into mourning." The odd little thief in the
glass globe is a symbol of vanity.*

lands, part of his personal program was to hunt out and acquire as many Bruegels as possible, and when he died these went to his brother, the emperor Rudolph II, king of Bohemia and Austria, a passionate collector who already had a number of Bruegels of his own. A third Austrian, Archduke Leopold Wilhelm, who died nearly a hundred years after Bruegel, was a third avid collector, which helps to account for the fact that Vienna is today unrivaled in its concentration of the Flemish painter's finest pictures.

Bruegel as a man certainly shared intellectually, if not by high birth, the aristocratic character of the men who during his life and long after his death were most interested in his painting. The sobriquet "Peasant Bruegel," attached to him in the sense of "the Bruegel who painted peasants," has misled a few romanticizers even in the twentieth century. And to his contemporaries outside the limited circle where his paintings were accessible, even to other artists and most commentators or historians, Bruegel was "Pieter the Droll" on the basis of those drawings for engravings that were published by Hieronymus Cock. "Pieter the Droll" was always thought

of as a follower of Bosch, which is much less than half the story.

Like Bosch, Bruegel treated things monstrous and deformed as symbols of moral corruption. But where Bosch's visionary intensity is concerned only with a nightmarish battle between the forces of heaven and hell, Bruegel never quite leaves the real world. There is always an admixture of humor with the grotesquery, and of compassion with the morbidity. Sin for Bruegel was more than a matter of private degradation: his most hellish conceptions are comments on the texture of society as well as moral abstractions. When he shows us maimed beggars dragging themselves along with rough sticks as crutches, their brutalized spirits showing dark and blank behind their eye sockets, he shows them to us not only as Bosch showed his monsters, as symbols of the spirit defiled by sin, but also as the victims of human cruelty. At a time when the maimed, the insane, the feeble-minded, and the deformed were laughed at, or at best thought of as animals differing from stray dogs only in being more diverting, Bruegel made them a rebuke to society. Without idealizing them or pretending that they were anything more than bestial, he said that they had been born men and that their reduction to a bestial state was accomplished by a cruel society that thus degraded itself.

Although in his early paintings Bruegel adapted freely whatever served him in the pictorial schemes of his predecessor, the two artists are not much alike in effect. Bosch's greatest work is calculated to induce an orgy of spiritual terror by way of an orgy of sexual excitement. But Bruegel's horror of sin has less to do with damage to the immortal soul than with the ignobility it inflicts upon the living man: foolishness becomes a greater sin than lust. Explicitly sexual references are rare in Bruegel's work, and suggestive sexuality does not exist in it.

Bruegel's revulsion for the follies of materialism might in another artist have produced nothing better than cynicism or ivory-tower withdrawal. Instead Bruegel was certain that a saving grace was bound within the scheme of life. He found it in the natural wisdom of the uneducated man, who might have only the cloudiest idea, if any, as to what the word "philosophy" meant, but who had built up a kind of catalogue of philosophical principles in the form of parables and proverbs.

The intellectual discovery of proverbs as statements not only pithy but profound was not unique with Bruegel. Erasmus, among other philosophers, had collected them. But they were the ideal subjects for Bruegel at just this moment. Their imagery was as fantastic as that of any symbols of sin, but their substance was sociological and humanistic rather than theological. Proverbs—whether in their condensed form as catch phrases or extended as parables—are usually self-generated from the life of the people, and they endure for the double reason of their solid truth and the novelty of their expression. Bruegel collected (in 1559) about a hundred Netherlandish proverbs and showed them all being acted out en masse in a Netherlandish village, thus producing in one picture a phantasmagoria, a compendium, a genre record of dress and physical types, and a kind of satirical ballet on the subject of man's infinite capacity to demean and defraud himself.

If the form of these proverbs is not always familiar to us, the meaning is—as the following examples prove: "Heads won't break walls" (it's no use butting your head against a stone wall); "He carries a basketful of light outdoors" (carrying coals to Newcastle); "An eel held by the tail is not yet caught" (don't count your chickens before they're hatched); and so on.

Bruegel's recognition of human foibles never reduced him to bitterness—or at least never to any discernible in his work. From the mass of it we can deduce that he regarded misanthropy as a form of self-interest as degrading in its way as avarice or gluttony. He said something of the kind in *The Misanthrope* (page 31), a painting not easy to decipher, where a stooped, sour old man plods through a landscape composed (like the

CONTINUED ON PAGE 41

32

PAINTINGS OF PEASANT LIFE

The five paintings below are among Bruegel's best known and best loved. Two are reproduced in full and the other three in detail in the following eight pages of gravure. The Harvesters is in the Metropolitan Museum of Art, New York; the other four are in the Kunsthistoriches Museum in Vienna.

Peasant Wedding, *circa 1567*

The Harvesters, *1565*

The Hunters in the Snow, *1565*

The Fight Between Carnival and Lent, *1559*

The Peasant and the Bird Nester, *1568*

CONTINUED FROM PAGE 32

world?) in the form of a circle. The old man has isolated himself within this world under a black cloak with a deep hood. We see only his long, drooping nose, his tight, turned-down mouth, and his dangling white beard; everything is hidden from him except the bit of barren path immediately beneath his lowered gaze, where a few thorns are scattered. He is oblivious to the deep landscape stretching beyond him (suggesting, as do so many of Bruegel's landscapes, the swelling curve of the earth), where a shepherd tends a flock of sheep—some black, some white—and a windmill turns. The misanthrope is not aware, either, of a bizarre, ragged little figure encased in a crystal globe (the world, again?), who has reached up under the cloak to filch the old man's moneybag. The misanthrope is doubly robbed: wrapped in the false security of his symbolic cloak and hood, he robs himself of the world—but he cannot escape the world even so, for it in turn robs him.

In Bruegel's picturizations of proverbs and parables the Netherlandish peasant is employed only as a pantomimist, but in the paintings of peasant life he comes into his own as Bruegel's symbol of significant man. Rejecting the elegant but now bloodless gods and heroes who continued to preen and posture in Italian mannerist art and its international offshoots, Bruegel could have fallen into the worse trap of sentimentalizing a lout as the symbol of virtue, making him equally bloodless in specious opposition to the Olympians. But he recognized the peasant as a frequent lout and often showed him as one, with an open and sometimes ribald humor that was neither jibing nor condescending. Bruegel prettified nothing. As far as detail is concerned, the peasant pictures are accurate genre records. A feast in a granary is an explicit description of the setting, of the paraphernalia (and table manners) of eating and drinking, and even, if you examine the faces individually, of village types.

But all detail is incidental to the generalization of form by which the commonplace becomes monumental: the village feast that begins as a genre scene ends as an expression of the richness of life. A wedding dance where the heavy-bodied men and women whirl in a mass that must have been sweaty and galumphing surges with the life force that for Bruegel was the invincible truth.

Like Michelangelo, Bruegel created a symbolic colossus from the material of the human figure. But the two artists' colossi resemble one another only in the monumentality of their weight and breadth. Michelangelo idealized man as the supreme intellectual and passionate force. The beauty of the idealized body in Michelangelo's art expresses man's spiritual nobility, but in its state of glorious nudity the symbol exists without earthly connections; it could never walk through the streets, could never inhabit a landscape that was not correspondingly invented to suit it.

In Bruegel all this is reversed. The symbol's majesty lies not in its beauty but in its plainness. Michelangelo's

Adam, the consummate expression of his ideal, may have been created from clay, but the fact is important only because it emphasizes the miracle of his gloriousness. Bruegel's man need not—must not—lose his identification with earth, for earth is not a base material. No matter that the body, wrapped in rough garments which belong to it as a pelt belongs to an animal, is clumsy by any standard of idealized form. In any form but its own, it would lose its identity with nature.

In his last years Bruegel returned to the celebration of nature in a series of pictures on the subject of the months of the year, recognizing but transcending the medieval formula that had produced hundreds of pictorial variations as different from one another as the illuminations in the *Très Riches Heures du Duc de Berry* and the crudest woodcuts in popular Shepherds' Calendars.

Bruegel sufficiently observed the conventional subject matter of the occupations assigned to each month, but his true subject was the mood and the feel and the look of nature in its cycle. Men are as natural a part of it as plants and lakes and fields, and like them, men are subject, beyond their will and for better or worse, to the permeating heat and brilliant light of full summer, to the blustery chill and lowering skies of November, to the frozen spareness of deep winter.

Painted about four years before his death, Bruegel's final visions of nature and man in nature are surely unexcelled by any paintings, anywhere, as expressive summaries of the natural life of our planet as it turns around the sun. But man's almost puppetlike subjection to the cycle is too easily interpreted as Bruegel's final conclusion. When he died, he was still painting peasant and religious subjects; he had barely abandoned the monsters that earlier had filled his work. If he was trying to reach some kind of conclusive statement of his complex philosophy, he had only begun.

Looking at his total work from the arbitrary boundary line of his death, we can make only a partial summary of his potential: for all its greatness, his total work was only work in progress. He had told us in various ways that man is one manifestation of universal force; also that he is only a tiny manifestation, and that nature is indifferent to his well-being, being neither malevolent nor benevolent; also, that when man breaks from nature, he becomes the victim of his own frailties. But Bruegel never accepted any human condition as proof that the cosmos is an accident—or that man's life within it is meaningless.

This ninth in a series by John Canaday, art critic of The New York Times, *is adapted from a section of his forthcoming book* Lives of the Painters (*W. W. Norton & Co.*).

For further reading: Bruegel *by Robert L. Delevoy* (*Skira, 1959*); Bruegel: The Paintings *by F. Grossmann* (*Phaidon-N.Y. Graphic Society, second edition, 1966*); Bruegel: The Drawings *by Ludwig Munz* (*Phaidon-N.Y. Graphic Society, 1961*).

IN THE LETTERS OF PETRARCH THE INQUIRING MIND OF MEDIEVAL MAN COMES TO LIFE. Horizon PRESENTS A SELECTION, TRANSLATED FOR THE FIRST TIME INTO ENGLISH BY MORRIS BISHOP

Petrarch, or Francesco Petrarca, whose likeness appears in the fourteenth-century illumination above, is one of the world's greatest poets. In his love-rimes for Laura he set the theme of the sighing swain hopelessly wooing an obdurate lady, and couching his woe in mellifluous sonnets. The theme dominated the European lyric even to our own day, when it was transformed into crooner's whine. As Petrarch advanced in years, he affected to despise his youthful poetic ardor, though he kept on revising the poems until his death. From a great poet he became a great scholar. In love with the Roman past, he was one of the initiators of the humanistic revival that was soon to become the Renaissance. His humanism was in accord with Christian faith. His younger brother Gherardo joined the Carthusians, severest of orders; Petrarch regarded his brother with affection mingled with envy, for Gherardo had gained an assurance of immortality that literature could not grant.

Petrarch had an original, inquiring mind. He was the first recorded Alpinist, who climbed a mountain merely for pleasure; he was one of the first to celebrate the beauty of wild nature; he was a mild archaeologist, a collector of Roman coins; he possessed the rudiments of scientific purpose. "I am anti-Aristotle whenever Aristotle is anti-common sense." He had a very unusual taste for introspection; he examined his own behavior with pensive delight. He is informative about the literary, ecclesiastical, and courtly worlds, about food, clothing, travel, medicine, gardening, and the routine of ordinary existence. He gives us in his letters the most nearly complete picture in existence of the inner and outer life of a medieval man.

He was a letter writer by instinct and early habit. When, in 1345, he discovered the unique manuscript of Cicero's *Letters to Atticus*, he recognized that genuine letters on everyday matters, Familiar Letters, constituted a literary genre that could comprise his own familiar letters. He collected and edited them, discarding some, revising others, possibly even creating some anew. His busy secretaries kept copies of his outgoing correspondence up to the time of his death.

The bulk of the letters, in the original Latin form, is enormous. Many of them have not been reprinted since the sixteenth century. Only a few have hitherto been translated into English. The letters that follow are from a selection published by the Indiana University Press under the title *Letters from Petrarch.*   MORRIS BISHOP

On his brother's life in the Carthusian monastery of Montrieux, with recollections of youth and exhortations to piety

TO HIS BROTHER GHERARDO, FROM CAPRI (NEAR MODENA), 25 SEPTEMBER 1348 OR 1349

My dear brother, dearer to me than the light of day, I am impelled to break my long silence. And if you think that was caused by my forgetful spirit, you are much mistaken; I would no sooner forget you than my own self. I was reluctant to interrupt the peace of your novitiate; I knew well that you were in love with silence, that you were fleeing all disturbance. And I knew that if I should once begin to write, I shouldn't easily stop, such is my love for you and my admiration for your course. So between two extremes I chose not the one that would give me most pleasure but the one that would leave you most peace. And now, to tell the truth, I am writing not so much for your pleasure as for my own. For what need have you of my prattle, you who have set foot on the celestial way, who rejoice in converse with angels? Happy are you, blest in purpose, who could in the prime of life spurn the world's allurements when they were most compelling, who could stop your ears and safely pass the siren voices. So while I am writing to you I bring myself advantage, for perchance my heart, sluggish and chilled with long inertia, may be warmed by your holy ardor. . . .

You remember how strong and how foolish was our desire for fine clothes, which still amazes me, though less as time goes on. What endless boredom and bother of putting them on and putting them off, morning and evening! How we feared that a hair would be displaced, and that a breeze would upset the proper structure of our coiffure! How we had to dodge the animals coming every which way in the streets, so that our perfumed, spotless gowns wouldn't get a splash of mud or have their folds disarranged by jostling! How vain are men's cares, especially young men's! Why all this anxiety in our minds? To please the eyes of others. Well, whose eyes? Those of a lot of people who found no favor in our own eyes. Seneca says in a letter to Lucilius: "Who ever put on a purple gown, except to show it off to somebody else?" It's idiocy to regulate our lives not according to intelligent reason but to suit popular fads, and to call in as judges of our lives those whose own lives we despise. No one chooses for a captain someone with a sword wound on his back, or for pilot someone famous for his shipwrecks. We choose those we admire, and we trust our business to those who have brilliantly handled their own. And so to follow the fashions of the vulgar mob, whose manners we laugh at and whose lives and opinions we despise, is to be more idiotic than the mob.

To continue my argument, let ambition cease and let the mob go its own way. A commoner's costume is more useful, adaptable to circumstances, and practical than that of a king. But we thought quite differently in those days. We thought it worth any trouble to be looked at, and, as Persius says, to have people point at us and say: "There he goes!"

Horace was a celebrated writer, but more fastidious than a man should be. He was as particular about his appearance as about his literary style, and he never appeared in public without consulting his mirror. He would primp and admire himself in it, and compose his face and his toga before it. He displayed many unmanly ways. Once a colleague bumped into him in a crowded street, and in the collision dislodged the artfully folded toga from his shoulder; and with truly feminine vanity he brought an accusation of injuries, as if an offense to a beautifully ordered gown were a capital crime. And, my dear brother, though we never brought suit for an injury of this sort, we were not far from it in spirit. However, you were suddenly changed by God's intervention, and were rescued from the darkness of such errors. But I am still struggling upward

with much effort; and I think it is granted to me to understand that there is no help in literature or in our own intellects, but all is the work of God, who will perhaps lend me his hand as I confess honestly my own helplessness. If reason did not convince me of this, I should be forced to recognition of it by old age, which every day I feel approaching nearer and already invading my domains.

And what shoes we wore! They were supposed to protect our feet, of which they were in fact the fierce and unrelenting enemies. They would have crippled me completely if, warned by extreme necessity, I hadn't preferred to shock other people rather than to squeeze my bones and sinews out of shape. And what of our curling irons and our artful locks, which cost us labor and pain and robbed us of sleep! What pirate could have tortured us more than we did ourselves! How often in the morning we saw red wounds on our foreheads, so that when we wanted to show off our beautiful hair we had to hide our faces! Such performances are agreeable to the actors, but distressing in remembrance, and incredible to those who have never indulged in them. As you recall our past silliness, how must the present delight you! Your loose sandals are not fetters to the feet but protections; your hair, close-clipped, no longer hangs like a hedge over your eyes and ears. Your simple robe, easy to care for, slips on and off readily, and thus defends the mind from folly as it does the body from cold. How fortunate you are that you endured all those annoyances as a preparation for your present commodities!

I shall skip other minor matters; but to make you the more thankful to God for rescuing you from our sea of troubles, I should like to recall how late we watched and how hard we worked so that our folly should be widely known and so that we might become the town's talk! How we would distort our pronunciation and upset the normal word order! In short, what didn't we do so that our affectations, which we should properly have rooted out, should be applauded and admired! We were praised for our zeal; "the oil of the sinner anointed our foolish heads." But God's ineffable pity directed your steps little by little toward the right road and chastened your rash impulses, sending disgust with all transitory things, in order that you, who had at different times been a citizen both of Babylon and Jerusalem, might well learn the difference between the two. O merciful God, how silently dost thou counsel, how secretly dost thou come to our aid, how insensibly dost thou cure!

And O dear Jesus, how eagerly we sought out a love not merely mortal but mortiferous, whose deceptive sweetness, mixed with pain, thou didst permit us to taste, lest in ignorance we should think it very fine! And in thy great mercy thou didst ordain that our loves should not overwhelm us; for thou didst remove the objects from this world; and thus with thy hand thou didst eradicate our hope when it had barely taken root.* Thou didst summon

*The reference is to the death of Petrarch's beloved Laura in the Plague of 1348.

them in their youth; and their death was, I hope, useful to them, as it was necessary for us, when thou didst strike off the fetters of our souls. And yet—O mortal blindness!—often we lamented their premature passing, whereas their life was prolonged to the prejudice of our own. As if what is salutary could be untimely!

What sighs, what laments, what tears we cast to the winds! And how, like madmen resisting their physician, we thrust aside thy hand, which sought to apply thy sovereign balm to our wounds! Now, Gherardo, tell me, you who have changed from God's enemy to his friend, from his adversary to his citizen, tell me, since you have revised all your judgments, what resemblance is there between our silly songs, full of false and indecent praise of loose women and shamefully revealing our lusts, and those sacred chants and midnight vigils with which you prepare your assault on the ramparts of God's holy city and sleeplessly resist the crafts of the ancient enemy! It is a blessed and enviable army. The labor is hard, I admit; but it will be brief, and it will merit an eternal reward.

Now there is one thing, dear God, on which I should like to ask counsel, if thou dost permit. Since my brother and I were caught in the same snare, why, prithee, did thy hand smite us both alike, but why then were we not both set free? He arose; but I, when the snare dropped, was still so besmeared with the lime of evil habits that I cannot spread my wings. Where I was bound I now stand released but motionless. Why, when "the snare was broken and we were escaped," did not the sequence follow, of "our help in the name of the Lord"? We had begun this Psalm of David with sweet harmony; why did we conclude it with such dissonance? The will of God always has its reasons, since all men are subject to it, and since it is the origin of all causes. My brother then properly uttered his song, with his spirit uplifted to heaven. But perhaps I did not perceive the liberating hand, or perhaps I trusted in my own powers; for such a reason or another, though my snare is broken I am not free. Have mercy upon me, O Lord, that I may be worthy of thy further graces; for without thy free grant wretched humanity can in no wise obtain mercy.

The dismal trade of schoolmastering

TO ZANOBI DA STRADA, A FLORENTINE SCHOOLMASTER AND POET; FROM AVIGNON, 1 APRIL 1352 (OR PERHAPS 1349)

. . . Let them teach who can do nothing better, whose qualities are laborious application, sluggishness of mind, muddiness of intellect, prosiness of imagination, chill of the blood, patience to bear the body's labors, contempt of glory, avidity for petty gains, indifference to boredom. You see how far these qualities are from your character. Let them watch boys' fidgety hands, their wandering eyes, their *sotto voce* whisperings who delight in that task, who enjoy dust and noise and the clamor of mingled prayers and tears, and whimperings under the rod's correction. Let them teach who love to return to boyhood, who are shy of dealing with men and shamed by living with equals, who are happy to be set over their inferiors, who always want to have someone to terrify, to afflict, to torture, to rule, someone who will hate and fear them. That is a tyrannical pleasure, such as, according to the story, pervaded the fierce spirit of that old man of Syracuse, to be the evil solace of his deserved exile. But you, a man of parts, merit a better occupation. Those who instruct our youth should be like those ancient authors who informed us in our own early age; as those who first aroused our young minds with noble examples, so should we be to our successors. Since you can follow the Roman masters, Cicero and Virgil, would you choose Orbilius, Horace's "flogging master"?

What is more, neither grammar nor any of the seven liberal arts is worth a noble spirit's attention throughout life. They are means, not ends . . .

Cicero wounds his leg

TO NERI MORANDO, A VENETIAN OFFICIAL; FROM PAGAZZANO, NEAR BERGAMO, 15 OCTOBER 1359

. . . Listen to the trick Cicero played on me—Cicero, whom I have loved and cherished since boyhood! I have a great volume of his letters, which I wrote out some time ago with my own hand, since it was too hard for the scribes. (My health was then poor, but my love and delight and eagerness to possess the book surmounted the body's incommodities and made light of the toil.) As you have seen, I kept the book standing on my library floor, right next to the door, in order to have it always at hand. So then I came into the room, thinking of something else, and the edge of my gown happened to catch on this book. It fell down, and gave me a slight wound on the left leg, not much above the heel. "What's this, my Cicero?" I said. "Why are you wounding me?" He didn't say a thing; but the next day when I entered the room he smote me again, and jokingly I put him back in his place again. Well, to cut it short, I was repeatedly injured and taken by surprise; and as he seemed to be angry at standing on the floor, I put him higher up. But since the skin was broken by the repeated blows on the same place, the sore was not to be disregarded. However, I did disregard it, judging rather by the petty cause than by the actual case. Thus I didn't stop drinking water, or horseback riding, or walking. You can imagine the result. As if angry at being neglected, the wound swelled, and a kind of discolored, infected flesh gathered about it. So finally when the pain became no laughing matter and disturbed my sleep and repose I realized that my neglect was not elevation of spirit but mere folly.

So I called in the doctors. They have been treating the now serious wound for many days, causing much pain, and with some danger, they say, of injury to the limb. Although you know, I think, how little faith I put in their prognostications, good or bad, I must suffer frequent fomentations, abstain from my usual food, and keep my body in a very unaccustomed inertness. All this I hate; especially being forced to eat dainties that would delight a gourmet.

But now things are going better; you will hear news of my convalescence rather than of my illness. One thing irritates me, that almost every accident, every ailment, lands inevitably in that one part of my body, so that with good reason my servant, doing his humble duties, often jokingly calls it my unlucky leg. It has often bothered me, through my whole life. It has forced me, from boyhood on, to spend a good deal of time lying quiet, a thing I dislike above all else . . .

The pleasures of writing in old age

TO BOCCACCIO;
FROM PADUA,
28 APRIL 1373

. . . I am conscious of the love that prompts you to give me medical advice, although you don't heed it in your own case. Please pardon me if I don't obey you. Even if you did convince me, as if I were very eager to live longer, as I am not, I should die the sooner for following your advice. Constant, persistent labor is the food of my mind. When I begin to slow down and to take repose I shall soon cease to live. Reading and writing, which you tell me to reduce, are only a slight task, or rather they are a pleasant relaxation that makes one forget serious labor. Nothing weighs less than a pen, nothing is more cheering. Other pleasures flee and leave depression behind; but a pen allures you when you take it up and delights you when you lay it down. And it profits not only its master but often many others who may be far off, and sometimes even men of the future, thousands of years away. I think one may properly say that of all earthly delights none is more noble than literature, none longer-lasting, sweeter, more constant, none that so readily endows its practitioner with a splendid cloak for every circumstance, without cost or trouble. So forgive me, my dear brother, forgive me; I shall believe you in all else, but not in this advice of yours. You may draw of me what picture you please—for there is nothing that the pen of a true literary man cannot do—I must continue to struggle on my way. If I am nothing I must strive to be something; if I am something I must try to be a little more; if I were great, as of course I am not, I should do my best to become greater and greatest. May I not borrow the phrase of Maximin, that monstrous barbarian emperor: "the greater I shall be the harder shall I work." The remark was worthy of one not a barbarian.

So that point is settled. You will learn from the letter that follows this one how far I am from accepting counsels of inactivity.*

Not content with the extensive works I have begun, for which this short life cannot suffice, nor could it suffice if doubly as long, I keep hunting out new, additional tasks, such is my hatred for sleep and languid repose. You must have heard the verse from Ecclesiasticus: "When a man hath done then shall he begin: and when he leaveth off, he shall be at a loss." It seems to me that I have only just begun. However I may appear to you and to others, that is my judgment on myself. If my life should end at any moment now, and certainly it cannot be much prolonged, I could wish that my work could be completed with my life. But since that is too much to hope for, I hope that death may find me reading or writing, or, if it be Christ's will, praying and weeping. Farewell, my friend; do not forget me; and live your happy and manly life.

*The letter that followed contained a translation of Boccaccio's *Griselda* into Latin.

BRESLAU REVISITED

An American who studied there
before the days of Hitler returns to a
city with another name,
filled with people of another culture
and another tongue

By FRANCIS RUSSELL

It is a name expunged from the maps. Five hundred thousand inhabitants of Breslau, the old Silesian capital, have long since been driven out, replaced by strangers of another culture and another tongue. German Breslau has become Slavic Wroclaw. The baroque university buildings by the Oder now house a Polish state university. It is not given to many of us to have lived in a city that no longer exists. But it was given to me in my student time in Germany.

I think most of us develop a certain nostalgic affection for the place where we were first undergraduates. For me there has been an even more poignant groping for the past, since the Breslau student world I knew—however exact my memories—has been obliterated. Often after the Second World War as I have wandered about my native Boston, its central area the size of my lost German student city and with only a slightly larger population, I have found myself wondering how this present American city would seem if it had suffered a similar overturn. Walking down Beacon Street past the gilt-domed State House to-

ward King's Chapel, I have tried to imagine what it would be like if the variegated crowd I saw milling along the sidewalks and violating pedestrian traffic regulations were replaced by more uniform and orderly foreigners, if the familiar landmarks from the Jamesian Athenaeum to Raymonds' Where-U-Bot-The-Hat had been emptied and put to other uses, if the State House offices behind Bullfinch's classical façade had all been expropriated by an alien administration, if even the monuments in the Public Garden had been removed, so that nothing remained but a ghostly outline.

This was of course the fate of Breslau after the Nazis had turned it into a defensive fortress in the spring of 1945, after more than half its buildings had been destroyed in the assault by the Red Army, finally after Silesia with its capital had been handed over to the Poles as compensation for the eastern part of Poland that the Russians had annexed.

So a thousand years of German history vanished, unique as the pattern of Breslau itself was unique. For the pattern was

woven of curiously contrasting threads. Breslau was a German city founded by a Bohemian count with the Polish name of Wratislaw, who cared nothing about nationality. It was a gothic city and a baroque city, a city of the Reformation and the Counter Reformation, a free city of the Holy Roman Empire without the title of Free City, that gave its varied allegiance to Polish, Bohemian, and Hungarian kings. Under the Habsburgs it was the equal of Prague, and in modern times under the Hohenzollerns the second city of Prussia, a European as much as a German city, and the German gateway to the Slavic East. Three times Breslau was overrun by invaders: by the Mongols in the thirteenth century; six hundred years later by Jerome Bonaparte, who leveled the medieval walls and bastions; and finally by the Russian tank and infantry battalions at the close of World War II. And even now, the ghostly outline of the German Breslau has become the fourth city of Poland.

Breslau's history meant little to me when I arrived there first, a foreigner and a stu-

dent, on a gray afternoon in October, 1931, scarcely able to stammer more than a few phrases in the language that still eluded me as I heard others talking on the street. I knew no one. No one spoke to me. At the age of twenty I had the overpowering experience of being alone in a strange city, without the ingathering protection of dormitories, dining halls, and student unions. From the registrar's office, at the end of an eighteenth-century corridor intricate with scrollwork and painted allegorical ceilings, I received from a secretary a mimeographed address list of rooms for rent in private houses. With that I was on my own.

After a day's traipsing through unknown streets, and almost desperately, I took a room on the other side of the Oder in a blurred line of apartment houses on the Bismarckstrasse, a treeless boulevard bisected noisily by a streetcar line. Boulevard and block had a sullen aspect that carried over into the interiors. My small back room had brownish walls, liver-colored woodwork, and a single window overlooking an empty lot edged by yellow bitter

buttons and with a stunted birch tree at the far side. A red counterpane covered my bed up to its warped veneer headboard, and a bilious-looking tile stove stood in the corner. Against the wall was a commode with a chipped white washbasin and pitcher, near the window a wooden chair and a round table with metal claw legs that clutched spherical glass casters. Over the table a low-power light bulb hung from the fly-specked ceiling.

There was another student in the apartment who rented a front room, a shadowy figure whose footsteps I sometimes heard and whom I occasionally glimpsed as he emerged from the W.C. at the end of the dank corridor. The whole place smelt of drains and ancient food. My landlady and her widowed daughter looked enough alike to be sisters—heavy, rancid women with sweat-shiny faces, mouse-colored hair drawn back in tight buns, and red-rimmed pig eyes. They seemed to live in the kitchen, where at times I could hear a baby crying. Whenever I started to leave the apartment, the kitchen door would

open a crack as I passed and a blue pig eye would fix on me. Every morning the mother brought me my breakfast of rolls and coffee. She managed to double my bill each week by adding a list of previously unmentioned items—butter for my rolls, milk for my coffee, hot water for shaving, electricity, briquettes for the tile stove.

As I look back on those faceless weeks before the opening of the university term, they merge together in their loneliness. Day by day the air grew colder, the few remaining leaves fell from the stunted birch, the bitter buttons turned brown. Each day I sat at my ball-clawed table trying to teach myself German, reading Gottfried Keller's *Zurich Tales* or a selection of the fantastic stories of E. T. A. Hoffmann that someone had given me in England, looking up each word I did not know and writing it on a piece of paper. It wasn't, I later discovered, the best way to learn conversational German. Unwittingly I was teaching myself archaic phrases such as *"nichtsdestoweniger"* for "nevertheless" instead of *"trotzdem"*—which was like using "forsooth" in everyday English. In the bare lot outside my window I could hear the forlorn echo of a Salvation Army band—the *Heilsarmee*—that practiced there daily.

Late in the afternoon I usually left my books to explore the city that began gradually to assume a known and familiar pattern. As I walked down the Bismarckstrasse toward the Oder, the first thing I saw was the baroque university on the opposite riverbank, rising up ahead of me as out of a formal past, the sunlight glittering on the astronomical weather vane above the central tower. Come upon suddenly, the architectural profusion of those elongated buildings was overwhelming: Corinthian pilasters and scrolled lintels and truncated arches, cherubs perched on balconies or soaring over the heads of star-crowned madonnas, everywhere interlacing curves in a kind of petrified disquiet.

The street, with its trolley line, crossed the University Bridge to cut a tunnel directly through the baroque façade, a long, arched passageway known as the Kaiser Gate, which emerged on the other side at the cobblestoned University Place. To the left of this lopsided square stood a modern fountain topped by a statue of a naked fencer (a hazardous way to fence, it always struck me), while to the right the elaborate university portal with its columns, pilasters, and assorted balcony cherubs looked like a stage setting for *Don Giovanni*.

Breslau's center was the Ring, a quarter of a mile past the university, on the straight, continuing boulevard known as the Schweidnitzerstrasse. In spite of its name the Ring was a great square, surrounded by the elegant façades of late medieval patrician houses that served as a background for the Town Hall, the glory of the city and the most splendid secular building of the German Gothic. For all its towers and turrets and cusps and finials, it had an air of repose, almost of timelessness, as compared to the restless baroque university buildings. The late sun cut a soft reflection on stone and mellowed brick as I walked by, and always I stopped to admire the square clock under the flamelike traceries of the main

"My landlady and her widowed daughter . . . heavy, rancid women with sweat-shiny faces and red-rimmed pig eyes."

gable. That clock had a face like a radiant sun, and a single hand ending in a gilt, pointing finger balanced at its other end by a crescent moon. Around the corner from the clock was the double-doored entrance to the tavern rooms of the Schweidnitzer Keller. Two carved medieval figures flanked the entrance. To the left a husbandman, staggering home with a drinking cup in one hand and a pitcher of beer in the other, had stopped short at the sight of his angry, wimpled wife on the opposite side. She had taken off her shoe and held it menacingly as she advanced to settle accounts with him.

Nineteen thirty-one was the year of crisis, when one German male in three was out of work, when the brown shirts and the Red Front were fighting for control of the streets and Chancellor Brüning ruled without parliament on the strength of the desperate emergency decrees signed by the failing eighty-three-year-old President von Hindenburg. Even a stranger could sense the tension. At each corner of the Ring, news vendors had staked out their territories according to their politics, shouting their wares in hoarse, embittered voices. Near the Schweidnitzer Keller a pugnacious young man peddled the National Socialist papers, a swastika-trimmed tray suspended from his neck by a leather strap. On the other side of the Ring an equally pugnacious "proletarian" in a blue cap carried a hammer-and-sickle tray of Communist papers. A Nationalist, displaying the black-white-red banner of the Kaiser's time, occupied a third corner, and the last spot was taken by a Social Democrat, his tray decked with the miniature red-black-gold flags of the Weimar Republic that the Nazis called the mustard flag. A Ring bookseller had as his central window display a new book by the American journalist H. R. Knickerbocker: *Deutschland—So oder So? (Which Way Germany?)* Below the red title the dust jacket was divided by a black question mark with a swastika on one side and a hammer and sickle on the other.

One afternoon I watched a giant Communist parade wind past. Hard young men with swastika badges in their buttonholes stood ostentatiously on the corner jotting down the names of the marchers. Whenever

on my walks I heard the ululating wail of the police siren, I knew that another riot had broken out somewhere. Often I would catch a glimpse of the open-topped police van, the *Schupos* in their hard helmets sitting in rows like automatons, their rubber clubs at the alert. Almost every night someone in Germany was killed in the street fighting. In one of his emergency decrees Brüning had forbidden the wearing of uniforms—brown shirts, Red Front, the old soldiers' field gray of the Steel Helmets (*Stahlhelm*), the Reichsbanner green shirts made up of the Socialist youth defending the Republic, even the Boy Scouts. But one of the department stores on the way to the station, keeping just within the law, had a large window display of Nazi uniforms. It drew an enormous crowd. Each day I passed the equestrian statue of Frederick the Great, the bronze figure raising his protective arm over the province he had seized from alien Austria. Behind the proud king on his prancing horse I could see dark-edged autumn clouds gathering in the west, a symbol so it seemed of the storm rising over his Germany.

At the end of the month I gave up my dismal room on the Bismarckstrasse for an equally small but this time cheerful room at Monhauptstrasse 12, behind the Cathedral and the Botanical Garden, an address I had found on the university bulletin board. When I told my landlady and her daughter I was leaving, they spilled over in indignation and—perhaps to impress me —escorted me to their sealed parlor, a front room with a ponderous walnut cupboard, antimacassars on plush and walnut chairs, a whatnot with shells, and a bulbous center table beneath an opaque beaded lamp shade. Ropelike lace curtains masked the windows. It was as if the air had not been changed since 1912. Wilhelmine wedding portraits stared from the walls on each side of a wooden plaque onto which had been etched with a hot iron a romantic castle with birds flying over its towers; it was inscribed with the first line of Luther's hymn: "*Ein' feste Burg ist unser Gott.*"

It was against the law, the women told me in shrill duet, for any student to give up his room before the semester's end. I told them, knowing nothing about it, that two

"An inner court led me to the massive outer door over which was carved a stone Medusa's head."

weeks' notice was all I legally needed to give. "Monhauptstrasse," the mother muttered, her lips twisting in derisive contempt when she heard where I planned to go, "*ja, ja*, a very elegant, a very *vornehm* street!" Then the daughter exploded: "Our other student, Herr von Janowski, has been with us two years, and *he* is noble!" Although they threatened to sequester my luggage, I left at the end of the month.

My new landlady, Frau Lieb, was a gentle person with white hair and finely modeled features marred somewhat by the beginnings of a goiter. She asked me, and I agreed, to take my meals with the Lieb family. Her husband looked almost like a *Punch* caricature of a German, for he shaved his head and the fat at the back of his neck overlapped his collar. One of my more comic memories is of our Sunday dinners, with Herr Lieb screwing his monocle into place before carving the roast. Before the First World War he had been a factory owner in Kattowitz, a man of wealth and position. Frau Lieb still had letters of thanks that they had received from Admiral von Tirpitz after he had been their house guest. But the Liebs had lost their money in the aftermath of the war, and he had lost his factory when the Poles seized Kattowitz with the rest of industrial Upper Silesia in 1919. Without possessions, he had taken his family to Breslau, where he had prospered modestly as a manufacturer's wholesale representative until the depression struck him down. When I moved into Monhauptstrasse 12, the Liebs had rented two other rooms to students, and with their sixteen-year-old daughter, Juta, were living in a single back bedroom. By this time Herr Lieb was reduced to going from shop to shop and from door to door peddling a small electric immersion coil for heating shaving water in a glass. It cost five marks, and he made a mark for each one he sold.

Frau Lieb once showed me a number of pieces of iron that looked like scale weights, which she kept in a drawer. On each was stamped "We Gave Gold for Iron." During the war Germans had been asked to give gold to the government and had received the equivalent amount in iron. The weights Frau Lieb showed me were for what she and her husband had given. These iron trinkets and the Tirpitz letters were all they had left from their Kattowitz prosperity. But for the rent money from their student rooms, they would have had to leave the Monhauptstrasse. Juta, in her next-to-last year of high school at the *Gymnasium*, had nothing further to look forward to than her diploma.

For all the grim signs of that portentous year, it was with my move to the Monhauptstrasse that my happy student period at Breslau began. The quarter where I lived was really an island in the Oder, the old ecclesiastical domain still marked by the twin spires of the brick Gothic cathedral. Each morning, with the fox terrier Lumpi, I would start down the broad oak staircase, highly waxed each week by the cleaning woman—the *Putzfrau*—to the peril of pedestrians. At the lower landing a brown-tiled inner court of geometrical pattern led me to the massive outer door over which was carved a stone Medusa's head. To the left a plaster wall-medallion displayed several naked, improbable cherubs fishing.

Through the decades the image of Breslau has persisted in my mind with such clarity that it is as if I could see my own self with Lumpi beside me on a frost-flecked morning walking down that sedate, long-vanished street. The double row of lime trees is bare, and the street—whatever crises may be going on indoors—still manages outwardly to look as it did in those high years when the Kaiser was challenging England for a place in the sun. At the cor-

"That clock had a face like a radiant sun . . ."

ner by the Botanical Garden I send the reluctant Lumpi home. He is a descendant of the wire-haired terriers that British officers of the occupation army brought with them after the war and that, unknown before in Germany, became fashionable in the twenties. I watch him once or twice to be sure he is not following me. There is rime on the garden's few remaining horse-chestnut leaves, and split pods and the intricately knurled chestnuts litter the pavement; the sun is beginning to melt the mist still hanging over the Oder. I can see the needle-spires of the cathedral almost detached by the mist from their solid brick base. At the end of the garden walk I turn into the narrow lane that leads me past the bulk of the cathedral. A nuthatch flies from its nest in one of the interstices of the high brick wall, twitters, and perches on a stone window ledge. The yellow baroque chapels extruding from the red brick apse look, as ever, incongruous; but time has given them a certain harmony of contrast. I skirt the cathedral square and pass the prince-bishop's palace where Cardinal Bertram lives; the fortresslike Church of the Cross where the medieval dukes of Silesia are buried; the baroque statue of John of Nepomuk, martyred fourteenth-century ecclesiastic, wearing his biretta and halo at a jaunty angle and looking as if he were about to take off for heaven on a stone cloud. Then I leave the cathedral island under the metal arch of the small bridge

that leads to the tiny Sandinsel almost overwhelmed by its looming Sandkirche. Past an intimate cluster of half-timbered houses, past the university library, I come to the morning bustle on the bridge that leads across the Oder and along the wide riverbank promenade. By the fencer fountain I wait the few minutes before my history lecture, hoping to run into Steffi who sits just ahead of me in the lecture hall. Students are thronging through the ornate portal now. Many of the men wear the Continental plus fours that come almost to their ankles. Nearly all the girls have switched to the new long skirts. Someone I met in the student *mensa* the day before nods to me. Pickering Pickering crosses the cobblestones, his dark, merry face intent on the lecture on Samuel Johnson that he is about to give and that he has cribbed from the *Cambridge History of English Literature*. He is an exchange lecturer from Birmingham, and he and I are the only native English-speakers in the whole university. At the moment he is trying to start a Foreigners' Club and stops to ask me to join. He received his odd double name because his mother's name was Pickering before her marriage—not, I thought, a very valid reason. While we are talking, one of our eccentrics passes, an older student from my history seminar with wing collar, black fingernails, and monocle, like some relic of the Free Corps volunteers from the early twenties—as perhaps he is. A bell tolls. At last I see Steffi coming from the direction of the Ursuline Convent where she has a student room, waving to me, a brisk figure in her Persian lamb coat, the high cheekbones of her half-Slavic face accentuated charmingly by her small cloche hat. The morning moment before the ornate portal endures, as if time itself had given a shrug and paused. Standing in the late autumn sunshine I have the feeling that the days cannot change, that the immediacy is too tangible. I shall always be here in an endless succession of mornings, my notebook under my arm, waiting for my friends.

Not until the end of November was I summoned to the rector to receive my student card. The formal matriculations took place in the Aula Leopoldina, a curved and cavernous hall where the baroque had exploded into the rococo. It and all the university buildings were survivals from the original Jesuit foundation built on the citadel of the Silesian dukes at the beginning of the eighteenth century. A Jesuit college of sorts had lingered there until 1811, when the king of Prussia combined it with the fading University of Frankfort on the Oder to form a new secular institution that he named, in honor of himself, the Frederick-William University. The Jesuit aula with its survival of form and color remained unaltered even to the marble bust of the emperor Leopold II in a cocked hat, which stood on what looked like a marble sarcophagus behind the rostrum. Nowhere in that restless room could the eye come to rest. Allegorical figures shot like skyrockets across the curved, painted ceiling; the river-god that was the Oder pursued the bosomy maiden figures of Breslau and Silesia; and over all the plaster exuberance of interrupted arches and scrollwork and trumpeting cherubs and sighing gods, above Urban VIII, Ferdinand III, Frederick the Great, and a long anonymous line of curators and rectors, Athena, the bare-breasted, mild-eyed Goddess of Wisdom, looked down in bewilderment.

Stern-faced in academic robes, the rector took his place on the platform with the bust of Leopold behind him. To his left lay the silver mace given to Frankfort on the Oder by Gustavus Adolphus, to his right the gilt mace presented by the founder, Frederick William III. One by one as our names were called we filed up for the ceremonial handshake and our student cards. We foreigners were the last batch to be welcomed, and I think the rector was getting a little tired of the often-repeated ceremony. I was the only American present in an exotic mixture of Indians, Swedes, Siamese, Turks, Bulgarians, White Russians, and even a delegation of Red Russians, who kept apart from everyone else and most apart from the Whites. The foreigners other than myself were in Breslau for sternly practical reasons, to study engineering or chemistry or medicine.

Steffi had told me to wear a stiff collar and a white shirt and to bow when I took the rector's hand. I think I had expected a friendly word as the sole American in the university, but the rector's face did not unbend as he grasped my hand in silence and with the same motion impelled me toward the exit. Elsewhere, as the lone American, I was almost a curiosity and soon came to know a number of students, including their politics. The year before, in the autumn elections, the Nazis had become the second largest party in the Reichstag. In any German university they would probably have won 70 per cent of the vote, certainly in Breslau. Once outside the shelter of the university, the students knew they were slated for a jobless world. National Socialism was the siren song promising them a future.

It was particularly ironic that the Nazis had won over the majority of the Breslau students, for it was here, after Napoleon's retreat from Moscow, that Frederick William had issued the "Appeal to My People" from his Palladian palace, and it was in the very Aula Leopoldina where we enrolled that Professor Henrik Steffens in 1813 made his fiery address to the students, calling on them to join the Free Corps to fight against the French and leaving his chair to go with them. Breslau students, then, were the first to raise the cry of freedom, and now, a little more than a century later, their successors were preparing to attack it with storm-troop daggers inscribed "Faithful to Röhm."

A solid minority of students still belonged to the old societies and on ceremonial occasions wore their corps uniforms. Each corps had three or four complete outfits, but the man had to fit the uniform, and I can remember in a dressing room of the university the comical sight of the corpsmen in their long underwear struggling to get into their tight breeches and almost thigh-high boots. Colored corps caps had almost disappeared for daily wear, although the duelist with cheeks so crosshatched by scars that he looked as if he had put his face through a windowpane was common enough not to attract attention. But the roistering student of the Old Heidelberg past—the pot-tossing, wenching August Beerkiller with his bright cap and his dog and his pipe and his stein and his wandering eye and his corps colors spread proudly

"The statue of Frederick the Great . . . the proud king on his prancing horse . . ."

across his chest—had been a casualty of the 1914–18 war. Out of a remotely innocent past had Brahms composed his *Academic Festival Overture* for the University of Breslau, and the Breslau professor-librarian with the birdlike head and bright eyes who called himself Hoffmann von Fallersleben had written the poem that would be the German national anthem, *Deutschland Über Alles.* Our times were grimmer and less musical.

Once or twice I went with a National Socialist student group to the Schweidnitzer Keller, where we sat at the heavy oak tables drinking beer in the low-ceilinged room under the brick outline of the gothic arches. The walls were decorated with the shields and monograms of the old Burschenschäften, the student societies stemming from the Napoleonic and 1848 freedom movements, who had drunk and sung there—Arminia, Cheruscia, Raczeks, Germania. Politics was our talk, and I heard over and over again about the crime of 1918 and listened for the dozenth time to the explanation of the National Socialist Führer Principle, which sounded to me merely like doing what you were told and no lip. Perhaps I appreciated it the less because Dr. Thompson, my old headmaster at the Roxbury Latin School, had developed the Führer Principle long before Hitler had ever thought of it. I also learned of the

National Socialist economist Gottfried Feder and of his illuminating distinction between *raffendes* (grasping) and *schaffendes* (creating) capital. A *raffener* capitalist apparently was one you didn't like, preferably a Jew; a *schaffener* was an industrialist who contributed to the party. Some of the students who took the socialism of National Socialism seriously talked of dividing up the large department stores. Such a giant seven-story steel-and-glass monopoly as Wertheims's they planned to split up and partition into a series of single-proprietor shops like booths at a fair.

Just before Christmas the kiosks blazed with posters announcing that Hitler was coming to Breslau to speak at the Jahrhunderthalle, the vast domed hall on the city's outskirts that had been built in 1913 to mark the hundredth anniversary of the Breslau-inspired rising against Napoleon. I planned to go out of curiosity to see this demonic man who was making a volcano of Germany, but Steffi said No. "You are not going to pay six marks for a ticket," she told me, "and help That Man." She always referred to him that way, and she was adamant. Later I saw the other Nazi leaders in the dock at Nürnberg, but the gutterman of destiny whom I failed to see at Breslau I was never to see.

As the days drew in, the Continental winter seeped across Silesia from the Russian steppes. One morning I saw frost blossoms in the Oder. A week later the river had frozen up in jagged chunks of ice. With the cold, the crisis deepened. Borsig, the great heavy machinery company of Berlin, closed down, with all its branches, and many of the workers and office help walked home crying. The sullen lines waiting in front of the *Arbeitsamt* to have their unemployment cards stamped grew longer. Even at the *Kindelmarkt*, the Christmas Fair, with its lights and tinsel-trimmed booths, one noticed the ominous note creeping in. At the confectionery booths they sold hard, thin gingerbread cakes trimmed with white-icing inscriptions appropriate for giving to children or to one's girl. I remember passing one stall piled a yard high and two feet across with cakes inscribed with the verse: *"In diesem Jahr wird's nicht so gross/Weil, Liebling, ich bin arbeitslos"* ("This year it will not be so big/Because, my dear, I am out of work").

At the thin end of the afternoon I often went home the longer way, through the cold glitter of the New Market, with its Neptune Fountain, where the *Kindelmarkt* was held and into the shadowed web of alleys where the narrow houses seemed to bend over the cobbles toward each other. Here under the cold street lamps the prostitutes walked their beats, their heels clicking sharply on the pavement. Occasionally a man would stop to bargain furtively with them. In appearance these walkers of the streets seemed middle-aged, like pensioned Sadie Thompsons, for they wore high-laced

Herr Lieb, "almost like a *Punch* caricature of a German," who voted, in despair, for Hitler.

black boots, checked skirts, and leather coats. The elderly men who bargained in the shadows were undoubtedly gentlemen of Edwardian tastes. I heard that the standard fee in the alleys was two marks.

I suppose at the age of twenty I felt a certain pleasantly vicarious sense of wickedness in hurrying through those grotesque lanes on my way to the lower bridge and past the Botanical Garden to the warm quietness of our Monhauptstrasse flat. If I was late, Frau Lieb kept my meal warm. She always managed to do small things for me. I would find my bedroom slippers filled with the traditional hard spice-biscuits known as *Pfeffernüsse* on St. Nicholas Day, a potted hyacinth on my desk for my birthday. The way she darned the heels of

my socks was not darning but weaving.

As the weeks passed and German began to form a fixed, accustomed pattern in my mind, the lectures I attended became less an exercise in patient incomprehension and more a matter of interest. Professor Mercker's lectures on Goethe I enjoyed most, although not always for reasons he would have appreciated. Round-faced, pot-bellied, beaming with enthusiasm for his subject, he devoted the first semester to the young Goethe and in particular to the Strasbourg student who rode along the banks of the Rhine to Sesenheim, where Friederike Brion, the pastor's daughter, waited for him. The Sesenheim lyrics that Goethe wrote to Friederike were the beginning of modern German poetry, as important to the language as Luther's Bible translation. Explaining that Goethe had composed his lyrics on horseback to the rhythm of his horse's hoofbeats, Mercker, quite carried away, recited *"Es schlug mein Herz. Geschwind, zu Pferde!"* with a rhythmic motion as if he himself were bouncing pudgily in the saddle from Strasbourg to Sesenheim.

Besides going to lectures, I practiced German by translating pages from *The Oxford Book of English Prose*, and almost every afternoon I sat for an hour or so with Steffi at the Four Seasons Café while she corrected my grammar and phrasing. Saturday afternoons we left books and grammar behind us. If the weather was bad, we visited the museums or the churches or such historical buildings as Frederick the Great's Palace where his grandnephew, Frederick William, had originated the Iron Cross in 1813. In clear weather we walked along the Oder, so far out beyond the city that the very spires sank away into the gray winter horizon and there was nothing but a frosted landscape, scattered low peasant houses, and a scarlet sun setting in the west. Once as we trudged back toward the city in the fading afterglow, a flock of rooks—seed-crows, in German—flew over and Steffi recited Nietzsche's mourning song for winter, his poem about the crows cawing in flight, perhaps the most austerely melancholy landscape poem in our Western culture.

I was late getting back to the Monhauptstrasse that evening, but Frau Lieb had kept my meal ready for me. "Here is the prodigal son," she said as I came through the hall entry into the dining room. In the artificial light our dining room looked opulent with the heavy silver service on the massive oak sideboard and the large landscape painting behind it. Actually the painting was an amateurish copy of one by Max Slevogt which hung in the Breslau Museum, and the silver service wasn't really silver but a nickel-plated set that Frau Lieb had picked up for a few marks when the Hamburg-American line went bankrupt just after the war. At close range one could see the HAPAG stamped on each piece.

My pink-calcimined room with the English sporting prints on the wall, my placid morning walks across the ecclesiastical island, the eighteenth-century lecture halls where I sat, the apple tart and whipped cream served with my grammar lesson at the Four Seasons, were an insulation against the stark alternatives of the disintegrating world outside. Yet with the opening weeks of 1932 I could see that the political pot was about to boil over. In March, President von Hindenburg's seven-year term was to expire and there would be new elections. The *Völkischer Beobachter* and other Nazi papers were already proclaiming that Hitler must be the next President of the Reich. In the last election the kaiser-true field marshal Von Hindenburg had been the candidate of the right, of the Nationalists, the Monarchists, and all those who preferred the black-white-red flag of Imperial Germany to the Weimar Republic's black-red-gold. But in a run-off vote the field marshal had defeated the candidate of the center and of the moderate Socialists, Dr. Wilhelm Marx, by only nine hundred thousand in a total of more than thirty million. It was the Communists who had really elected Von Hindenburg, for if they had thrown even a fraction of the two million votes to Dr. Marx that they had given to their party hack, Ernst Thälmann, Von Hindenburg would have been defeated. Now, in an ironic turnabout, the center and the moderate Socialists were supporting the kaiser-true marshal who, to the dismay of his rightist followers, had kept his

oath to preserve the Republic; the disgruntled Nationalists were running the leader of the *Stahlhelm*, Colonel Theodor Düsterburg, against their repudiated chief; Hitler was making his ferocious bid; the Communists, still refusing to co-operate in defending the Republic, had once again picked Thälmann; and there was even a freak candidate by the name of Gustav Winter, known as the thousand-mark man, whose sole and single platform was to redeem all the thousand-mark notes of the Kaiser's time that had been made invalid after the postwar inflation of 1918–1923.

The marshal-president's granite features stared down from every kiosk, framed in

Juta Lieb, born in better days, "had nothing further to look forward to than her diploma."

black-red-gold and bearing the quotation from Schiller, "Faith is the Mark of Honor." Communist posters showed heroic workers of weight-lifter proportions breaking chains. Swastika signs blanketed Breslau like swirling Catherine wheels. Belatedly, the Social Democrats formed what they called the Iron Front from the younger members of the Reichsbanner. The Iron Fronters went round with black crayons drawing three arrows through each postered swastika as if they were cancelling stamps. The kaiser-true marshal was bitter medicine for the Socialists, but he as Aesop's President Log was infinitely preferable to Hitler as President Stork, or so I heard a Social Democrat speaker explain. The speaker's voice, nevertheless, lacked

enthusiasm and he insisted on referring to Hindenburg without the "Von."

Election day, March 13, 1932, fell on a Sunday, as was customary in Germany to give more people the chance to vote. It was also the end of the university semester and the day before I was to leave Breslau for good. Frau Lieb had a loin of pork and red cabbage for my last Sunday dinner—the two dishes I liked best. "Well," she said, as the four of us sat at table, "I went down bright and early and voted for our President von Hindenburg." Herr Lieb's jaw set and his monocle quivered slightly in his teutonic face. "I voted for Hitler," he muttered challengingly. I said nothing. Nobody said anything. At the end of the meal I went to my room and closed the door, still without speaking. A few minutes later there was a knock. Herr Lieb stood on the threshold without his monocle, his face apologetic, his eyes sad. "Herr Russell," he said, "I don't like the brown shirts either, even if I did vote for Hitler. But what else can a man do? Something has to change. Nothing can be any worse than the way it is now, nothing."

I left Breslau early the next morning for Prague, walking for the last time through the snow-stained city to the station. Political posters still glared from the kiosks, the Ring itself was ankle deep in pamphlets and cards and stickers. But Hitler, for the moment, had failed in his bold challenge, collecting only eleven million votes to Hindenburg's eighteen-and-a-half million. Thälmann and the Red Front managed to get just under five million, and the *Stahlhelm* Düsterburg half that. Only by a half of one percent did the Reichspresident fail to get the majority of the votes that would have prevented the now-required run-off election in April. Thälmann, whose refusal to co-operate with the Socialists in 1925 had elected Von Hindenburg, now, by again refusing to co-operate with the Socialists, had prevented his re-election. But in any case Von Hindenburg would win the run-off easily. It was, as the *Berliner Tageblatt* remarked, the triumph of reason.

So it was that I left Breslau and my first term as a German student casually, intending to return but never managing to see the flat Silesian landscape again before the name itself had vanished. Not until a third of a century later, in October of 1965, did I find myself at last on the track of my own past and headed for a land and a city that no longer existed. Driving across East Germany, I had had my troubles with border guards and officials; my books and magazines had been confiscated, and I had even been detained for a few hours in East Berlin as a suspected currency smuggler. Now I sat at one end of the long bridge between East Germany and Poland at Frankfort on the Oder while the gray-uniformed *Vopos*—the People's Police—brought out a mirror on wheels like a small reflecting gocart, which they pushed back and forth under my Volkswagen.

Most travelers fly into Poland, and those who drive usually cross the border by way of Czechoslovakia. At Frankfort the crossover traffic is negligible. While I waited, more than an hour, for my passport—which I presumed the *Vopos* were photographing—there was only one other car at the control point, a Mercedes belonging to some West German businessman returning from Moscow. I noticed a babushka doll on top of the briefcases in the rear seat. At the other end of the bridge the white and red Polish flag hung limply. The afternoon sunlight made a green reflection in the water, of the meadow grass on the bank of the Oder; I could see tangles of rusty barbed wire and, in the other direction, the brooding landscape of the German Democratic Republic. For me, since the time I first saw it in 1945, there has always been a sinister quality about that barricaded landscape. In the deceptive autumn serenity at the afternoon's end it reminded me again of the land of the Head Forester in Jünger's *On the Marble Cliffs*.

After the hammer and compass emblem of East Germany, the Polish eagle over the bridge seemed a symbol of freedom. Once across that span I could drive where I pleased, stay in any city, talk with anyone. Yet, as the guard at last raised the border barrier, I found it like a waking dream to return to this countryside, the lost lands of Silesia. More than nine million Germans had fled or were expelled from the eastern territories, while about half that number of Poles were brought in from the regions seized by the Russians to replace them. The new settlers, said Cardinal Wyszynski in Wroclaw, have not taken over a German possession but an old inheritance of the Polish spirit. Nevertheless, the newcomers have never been wholly at ease in a land cultivated for generations by Germans and in houses built by others. For every Pole of middle age has seen war and invasion, and knows how quickly a political accommodation can alter the map. Recently a West German synod of Lutheran clergymen urged the former German inhabitants to renounce their claims to the lost lands beyond the Oder—to the belligerent anger of the various associations of the expelled. The country of one's birth, said La Rochefoucauld, endures in one's heart as well as in one's speech.

What struck me at once on entering Poland was that there seemed to be more horses than people. Even in East Germany all the farming is done by tractor, and horses have disappeared. But in Poland machines have not even begun to replace the horse. Criblike horse-drawn carts were the only vehicles I passed on the road, where from the shoulders melilot and yarrow were beginning to encroach on the concrete. The potato harvest was almost over, and the smoke of the root fires rose in blue plumes into the deeper blue of the afternoon. The only people I could see were groups of peasants picking up potatoes, but whenever I drove through a village, the little blond children came out to wave at me—so rare was the sight of a passing car. In each town the churches had all been carefully repaired—whatever the other leftover damage from the war—although the once Lutheran churches had become Catholic. Formerly there had been three million Lutherans in Silesia; now only twenty-five thousand were left.

The Poles have been thorough in uprooting the nomenclature of the German past, from Gdańsk (Danzig) in the north to Wroclaw in the south. It must have been a formidable renaming operation not only for cities and towns but for villages, rivers, and mountains. Just in a city like Breslau it meant finding new names for thousands of streets, squares, boulevards, and stores. The German statues have been melted down or carted off, and only Latin ecclesiastical inscriptions allowed to remain. On the outskirts of Breslau the German cemeteries shattered in the 1945 attack have been left to the weeds, but in cities like Gliwice (Gleiwitz) all headstones with German names have been removed. At Bystrzyca (Habelschwerdt) the grave of the great Silesian poet Hermann Stehr has been plowed over and the house where he was born torn down.

Yet there are still some seven hundred thousand Germans scattered through the Poland that was once Germany. Most are Water Poles, apart from both countries, considering themselves German but speaking a German-Polish dialect. In my travels through Poland I kept coming across other Germans in out-of-the-way corners, the flotsam of a war twenty years over. One such I met as I was driving from Poznań (Posen) to Warsaw and stopped off at a flyblown restaurant near Lowicz. Since I know no Polish, an old German in a frayed sweater came over to my table to help me decipher the menu. He was, he said, a village carpenter and would have gone back to Germany if he could, but the borders were now sealed. Proudly he told me that he had served in the Kaiser's army in the First World War.

At Gliwice near the radio tower I talked with a Slavic-appearing but German peasant woman who had been digging potatoes in the field opposite, and on noticing the identifying D on the back of my car had come over to where I was standing. That tower marked the broadcasting station where the Second World War had begun with Himmler's staged attack. The peasant woman had been living three houses away, and on the day of the attack had seen the car filled with SS men wearing Polish uniforms come racing up the street and had heard the shots. They had all known the attack was a fake, she told me. But Germany was still her country and this was her home. The Poles, she complained, had taken her house and her field and even her sewing machine, and now she was forbidden to speak her own language. I could not make out why she was still there. The reason was clearer with a German nurse I met

"Through the decades the image of Breslau has persisted in my mind with such clarity that it is as if I could see my own self walking down that long-vanished street."

in Gorzów (Landsberg). She had been a nurse there during the war years, overwhelmed with work and staying on until it was too late to leave.

Late one evening from a darkened road I saw the lights of Breslau, and scarcely believing it, I came again to that city of my first student years. Orbis, the official tourist agency, assigned me to the Hotel Monopol, a pompous building that had somehow managed to keep intact all the overblown décor of the Kaiser's time. In the lobby plush and mahogany held sway. My bathroom was larger than today's modern hotel room, though where the white tiles had cracked or fallen out they had not been replaced, the faucets all dripped, and the plugs for the bathtub and washbasin were held in place with picture wire. The one innovation in my vast high-ceilinged bedroom was a radio. Downstairs the only innovations were the faces of the guests, most of whom had the shifty look of Central European traveling men. I noticed that the desk clerk—a bleached blonde—

used an abacus to add up the bills.

More than half of Breslau had been destroyed in the 1945 attack. Shortly after the surrender a group of professors from Russian-occupied Lemberg arrived to establish a new Polish university. "There were still bodies lying on the street barricades," one migrating professor wrote; "the streets themselves were blocked with rubble, many houses were still burning, and the city looked dead." Others of his party thought that the city could never be rebuilt and might as well be crossed off the map. Yet the Polish government, stubbornly meticulous, had gone ahead restoring historical buildings and churches of the old city with an extraordinarily sensitive exactness, and heedless of the cost.

Early next morning—a bright, blowing day with hoarfrost on the ground—I started out to find what traces I could of Breslau in Wroclaw. Beyond the Monopol, Frederick the Great's palace was still a bombed-out shell, with the rubble removed but otherwise not reconstructed at all. Seeing

its desolation, I found myself recalling a reception I attended at the palace in the long formal hall, the crystal chandeliers blazing with candles. I think it had something to do with Pickering Pickering's Foreigners' Club. Anyhow, all the foreign consuls were there, wearing their decorations. Unfortunately, the candles in the chandeliers created a cloud of smoke that rose to the ceiling and then gradually descended layer by layer until at the end of the evening we were immersed in it like a London fog. Also, the candles dripped. I noticed a young English vice-consul, who had made a snide remark about my accent, standing under a chandelier unaware of the hot wax running down the back of his dinner jacket. I let him stand there.

Now, strolling from the palace, past the Monopol, along the former Schweidnitzerstrasse to the Ring, I could sense how the atmosphere of the city had changed, as if the air itself had been brought in by truckloads from Warsaw. It was not just the Polish voices I heard, nor the Slavic faces, nor

55

even the incomprehensible street and shop signs. The basic rhythm, which is unique to each world city, had altered. Wroclaw was indeed a Polish city. Not that the Ring itself seemed outwardly very different. The Town Hall, only lightly damaged, had been completely repaired, even to the finger-pointing hand that still moved across the square clock's sunburst face. Only the Schweidnitzer Keller's figures of the tipsy peasant and his raging wife—that four-hundred-year-old guffaw in stone—had been removed by the Poles as "uncultivated." Beyond the Ring the twin baroque towers of the Gothic Church of St. Mary Magdalene looked unchanged, the ancient Poor Sinner Bell in its tower still rang the quarters, the fronts of the Ring's patrician houses had been restored to their earlier elegance. Frederick the Great's statue had of course disappeared.

At the University Place there was just such a crowd of morning students before the baroque buildings as in my time. The cobbles, the ornate portal, even the fountain with the statue of the fencer where I used to wait for Steffi, looked unaltered. The baroque aula, where in unwonted stiff collar I had bowed to the rector so long ago, showed no sign of the war. Its faintly musty academic smell still lingered. The bust of the emperor Leopold had been replaced by a red velvet banner embroidered in silver with the Polish eagle.

Whether that mean little room on the Bismarckstrasse where I read Gottfried Keller to the accompaniment of the Salvation Army band was still standing I did not care to find out. Destroyed, I hoped. But one more time I wanted to walk the old way, across the Sandinsel, past the cathedral, along the curved path by the Botanical Garden to Monhauptstrasse 12.

The cathedral, as I glimpsed it from the angle of the iron bridge, had been shorn of its spires, and the twin brick towers peered stumpily above the trees in their isolation. Otherwise, except for a few shell pits, it was unchanged, even to the baroque chapels that I had thought the Poles in their architectural purism might have removed. Nuthatches still built their nests in the interstices of the brickwork.

At first I could not recognize my old

street. The buildings on the corner had been blown up during the siege to give a free field of fire to the artillery. I had to consult my old map carefully to be sure that ul. Jana Matejki had once been the Monhauptstrasse. I could see other blocks of apartments missing as I looked up the street, like teeth broken from a denture. Under the screening double arch of still-green lindens, number 12—whether there or not—was not visible. I walked hesitantly under the trees, almost convinced that I should find no more than another hole in the ground.

But number 12, along with its neighbors, was still there—the magnolia that I had forgotten about still intact on the front lawn, an American red oak that I had never before noticed partially masking the façade. Although the house itself stood, most of the stone facing and lintels had been shot away, exposing the underlying brick. A shattered entrance gaped open where the door had been. As I crossed the pavement to the still-visible 12 shield, a woman with a child passed and spoke to me in Polish. Inside the doorless entrance the geometric tiles were cracked, the treads of the stairway—devoid of wax now—hollowed and splintering. Yet in the hallway with its peeled paint and fragments of posted bills the cherubs still fished on their plaster riverbank. I went through the court and the back entrance and stood at last looking up at the window of my old room. Even as I stood there in the narrow, littered yard I could sense that, for all the apparent emptiness of the house, eyes were watching me from behind curtains. A child on the fourth floor waved to me, and vanished in a burst of shyness as I waved back. Then a bent, black-shawled old woman came shuffling down the stairs toward me. She begged my pardon, speaking in the thick accent of rural Silesia, showing two front teeth—which seemed to be the only ones she had—of stainless steel. A German she was, she told me, living there with her daughter who was married to a Pole. The other tenants had seen me and feared that I might be the former landlord come to inspect his old premises. Sensing trouble, with the Polish uneasiness at being dispossessed that still

lies beneath the surface in Silesia, they had sent her down to sound me out. As she talked in her harsh, senile voice, she forgot her errand, and her accumulated bitterness spilled over. She hated Poland. Since she had lost a son fighting in the *Wehrmacht* for Germany, she could receive no dole from the Polish state. Yet stay she must. She had no place else to go. "Ah," she said finally, "I would think even East Germany a paradise if I could only get there."

Leaving her muttering and shaking her head, I walked to the oak tree and stood looking at the ruined entrance to number 12 where I had started off for the university on so many brisk mornings with Lumpi. Herr Lieb's drill-master voice rang in my ears. "Nothing can be worse than it is now," he had said to me the day he had voted for Hitler. And, as if in the pattern of Greek tragedy he had condemned himself in his own words, he was to die in an air raid in Hitler's war, and his wife and daughter and the grandchildren he was not to know were to become refugees wandering without friends or possessions across the scrap heap that had for thirteen years been the Thousand Year Reich.

The Liebs were as forgotten as the dog Lumpi, although their name meant "love," as nameless now as the street, the university, the city, the province. Only I under the oak remembered. Looking up at the jagged brick façade of my old home, I knew I should not come back again to Breslau. The rest was Wroclaw. Yet never could I or would I lose the actuality of my German past: myself in starched collar receiving my student card from the rector in the aula; Professor Mercker on his rhetorical rides to Sesenheim; Frau Lieb asking, "Where is the prodigal son?"; Frederick the Great's fairy-tale palace with the candelabra ablaze; Steffi and me walking back along the Oder while the cawing rooks flew over us into the scarlet twilight; or the Poor Sinner's Bell of St. Mary Magdalene sounding the quarters as I crossed the University Bridge on a frosty morning when time itself seemed to stand still.

Francis Russell, whose personal tour of the Rhine River appeared in the Spring, 1964, issue, is a frequent contributor to HORIZON.

BEHOLD THAT (slightly unkempt) TIGER!

PRINCETON

A campus revolution—social, racial, sexual, sartorial, and even academic—has overwhelmed the Ivy League. Here an alumnus looks at Scott Fitzgerald's old "country club"

By JOHN DAVIES

"Some day, I predict with great certainty, there will be an enthusiasm for learning in Princeton." —WOODROW WILSON

In 1944, at a conference of American college deans, an elderly dean reminisced about the last generation of postwar students; he warned his younger colleagues that they were in for trouble with the veterans of the Second World War. Like so many academic predictions it was logical, based on hard evidence, in line with long-range trends—and completely wrong. In no university was this so strikingly demonstrated as at Princeton. After the First World War Princeton went silly; after the Second it went serious. In 1918 the "real" Princetonians wouldn't let the military trainees sing "Old Nassau"; in 1946 the veterans took over Princeton from the "real" Princetonians.

The supremely crucial fact for American universities soon became apparent: the American people had made a cult of higher education. The changing character of our society, now so highly organized and mechanized, placed an increasing premium on managerial skills and scientific knowledge; a college education, for substantial accomplishment in American business life, has become an economic as well as a social necessity. The A.B. degree is now the passport to the good life, and the thought of *not* going to college is intolerable.

This desire was fueled by a tremendous boom, a period of sustained prosperity that, in contrast to the 1920's, lifted the real income of the middle and lower classes as well as the upper class. Just about any lower-middle-class family could now afford to send a son to college, if it really wanted to and he was willing to work. Added to this was the federal government's decision not only to pay for veterans' tuition and books, but to give them a generous living allowance—in effect putting them all on a handsome scholarship. Then there was a flood of scholarship money from corporations and foundations—so much that Princeton, in particular, has a certain amount of difficulty in giving it all away.

But all the money, all the desire in America, could not have got these recent suppliants past the admissions requirements of the twenties, which effectively limited the entering class to boys who had taken—not understood but taken—courses in Greek, Latin, and advanced mathematics and languages usually offered then only in private schools. By 1946 these shibboleths had been quietly dropped in favor of the standard high-school "college preparatory" program. Now Princeton was doing what Harvard had been trying since the thirties, hunting for academic ivory among the midwestern and western all-stars instead of among the impassive sons of the rich.

Finally, the key to college entrance was shifted from a mastery of the content of prep-school courses to an assessment of the student's aptitude for college-level courses; because there is no way of cramming for an aptitude test, another built-in prep-school advantage disappeared.

The result was a tidal wave of applications for Princeton and, indeed, all the "prestige" colleges. For a freshman class of about eight hundred, more than fifty-seven hundred completed applications are currently received from young men of character and ability, fully prepared to profit from the Princeton experience, and by all predictions able to pass the courses and go through to graduation. The director of admissions has suddenly become the director of rejections.

Among those rejected are what would have been the bottom third of the typical prewar class, admitted without evidence of academic promise or scholarship just because the college was planned around a certain size of class: the college needed their tuitions to balance the budget and their bodies to fill up the seats. If they flunked out or quit, the university tried to find transfers to pay their bills and occupy their beds. This collection of "dead wood," some two hundred strong, usually came from upper-class families; they joined the best Princeton clubs, and often went on to become captains of industry and community leaders. They were the undergraduates who set the patterns, sartorial and social and intellectual, for the whole campus, infected even the bright students with their indifference, and made the eager boys eager only to imitate their own blasé attitude.

Today, this bottom third of a prewar class has been replaced by a "top third" of bright, aggressive high-school graduates from all over the country. From 20 per cent of cowed scholarship boys waiting on table, the public-school element has grown to a majority of 60 per cent; now it seems to dominate the place, to set the tone. The diversity achieved is wonderful and exciting. There is no "Princeton look" any more, no Ivy look, no "we happy few, we band of brothers." Short, tall, skinny, fat, the boys look instead like graduate students—which is what most of them will become. As a result of the new selection policies, there are over four hundred schools represented in a typical class; more than half of the students are the only representatives of their respective schools at Princeton—but each was the "best" boy in his school.

But the university has changed in other striking ways. In the 1920's few Jews chose to seek admission to the close, inbred world of Princeton, and those brave souls

The prevailing style of undress, seen here in the university's Firestone Library, has become an article of faith to a generation more concerned with content than appearance.

who did were aware of—in fact, were told—what treatment to expect. Most preferred to go to the big state universities where they could be assured admission, could find a large group of their coreligionists, and could even join a Jewish fraternity (or be blackballed from it). The very brightest, of course, went to Harvard, with its policy of taking the best students regardless, although its president in the twenties publicly advocated a Jewish quota.

After the Second World War, Jews began to apply to all the "prestige" colleges. In the twenties there were about fifty undergraduate Jews at Princeton; now there are four hundred. To be honest, of course, these are the days of FEPC, with no religious questions or photographs on application blanks; tax-exempt status can be endangered and political protests made if a school valedictorian is turned down without obvious and sufficient reasons. And those who are admitted are by no means all *déraciné* Jews, either, with the close-cropped hair and the clipped accent acquired in prep school.

In keeping with its old characterization as "the northernmost of the southern colleges," Princeton before World War II was lily white. In 1947 two Negroes were quietly enrolled (although not, at first, to live on campus).

Now the university actively recruits Negroes as it used to recruit football stars, and this special effort produces perhaps a dozen in each freshman class, along with a handful of Africans who are similarly recruited. All of them live in the dormitories, are freely accepted in the social clubs along Prospect Street, and most have white roommates.

Nevertheless, the most obvious index of this heterogeneous, diversified, middle-class Princeton is the one that first strikes the eye—dress. In the twenties Princeton students, living in what was then a country village without women, dressed to the teeth to impress each other—because it was "done"—in a uniform that established one's position on the campus social ladder: a button-down collar, a small-figured tie, a single-breasted tweed sport coat, gray flannels, and white buckskin shoes. The flannels have given way to chinos and the tweed coat to a crew-neck sweater, a gray shirt taken from the gymnasium, or a Harry Truman type of sport shirt; the white buck shoes may be GI boots (or in warm weather filthy white sneakers); and the whole ensemble is now topped off with a military parka. The campus, then, presents nothing so much as the appearance of a walking Army surplus store

*F. Scott Fitzgerald remembered the Ivy Club (opposite) as "detached and breathlessly aristo-
cratic," but a new egalitarian atmosphere now pervades its dark-paneled inner sanctuary, and
casually dressed members linger over lunch with a visitor from Sarah Lawrence College. Meanwhile, living conditions in the university's dormitories (above) reflect the curtailment of jani-
torial services (for economic reasons), as well as the students' more informal approach to dress.*

or, rather, a *used* Army surplus store. Occasionally one
sees Levis with high-heeled cowboy boots and sideburns
or even a Marlon Brando black leather jacket. In the
spring, or thesis-writing season, beards sprout; a great deal
of Princeton hair today is long and uncombed, with a few
semi-Beatle coiffures in evidence.

Started as a fad by returning servicemen, this style of
dress—or undress—is now an article of faith; but what it
represents is something else, and difficult to explain. It is
easy to attribute the unwashed visage of today to the in-
flux of young men without allowances to spend on clothes,
yet the prep-school element—still almost half of the student population—dresses in the same manner. This is
leveling with a vengeance. In any case, it is cheap, easy,
and in the spirit of Thoreau—one less thing to worry
about.

On weekends and at "Bicker" (the rushing period,
when the eating clubs select new members from the
sophomore class), the Madison Avenue look is broken out,
exactly as it was before the war, except that the lapels
have been narrowed, making old suits appear vaguely
obsolete; the button-down collar remains unassailable, but
the ties, of the same old challis material, have been nar-

rowed, too. Shoes are the same, except for a trend to
cordovan. But one senses that this is a one-suit, one-sport-
coat crowd, with no real interest in clothes. J. Press has
moved away, as has Frank Brothers, and the remaining
Ivy tailors put out ready-made "economy" models for the
student trade, making their real money out of the alumni
—and men who want to look like alumni.

A counterpart to this new sartorial grubbiness is a progressive deterioration of living standards. The university
has expanded by about six hundred students and has
brought the substantial number of freshmen who used to
dwell in boardinghouses onto the campus. Even with the
new dormitories, there are still more beds in the same
number of rooms, and some of them are double-deckers.
At the same time, rising maintenance costs led the university to abandon janitor service, with the predictable result that most of the rooms wind up somewhere between
being just plain dirty and constituting an active menace
to public health.

Another sign of the passing of the country club atmosphere is the progressive drying up of the town bars. The
old Princetonian, away from home, prep school, and
family, floated gaily on a sea of alcohol. But the use of

No longer does the sight of a skirt on the Princeton campus raise windows and shouts of "fire." Today the university's student body includes a number of married men with families, many more undergraduates who do their own laundry (center), and "a veritable army of dates" whose presence on campus (far right) and even in the dormitories is taken for granted.

alcohol is an index of social background; if the upper-class cocktail culture accepts and depends on it as the great social lubricant, the sober, hard-working, church-going middle class has always regarded it with suspicion. The Nassau Tavern, which used to tap sixteen half-barrels of beer a day before the war, now opens eight a week; the sacred Yankee Doodle Taproom, where one used to fight one's way to the bar through broken glass and hoarse singing, has a television set, a few middle-aged viewers, and women customers in its formerly all-male precincts.

Perhaps there is some obscure connection between heavy drinking and the absence of women. In the old days Princeton was a monastery into which females were imported three or four times a year; at any other time the sight of a skirt raised dormitory windows and howls of "Fire!" Now skirts are everywhere, and there is no more forceful impression than of the constant, all-pervading presence of women. There are many women on the research staff and even a few in the teaching force. The graduate school accepts women in special instances, and there are even a handful of female undergraduates, who transfer to study exotic languages for a year or two before

returning to their own campuses. Then there are several dozen undergraduate wives, since students can no longer be prevented from marrying.

Most striking of all is the army of "dates." American youth has gone "monogamous," according to one college president, and there is less playing the field. Women can remain in student rooms until midnight on Saturdays, a rule honored in the breach, and in this day of the Pill the only restraints are those of conscience. And of conscience there is little. The sexual revolution has blown across the nation's campuses, uprooting conventional standards and substituting the assumption that the only really deep relationship must include a sexual one. The undergraduates now cry that Princeton is a social desert because it is too far from the women's colleges for a one-night stand, and the *Daily Princetonian* earnestly and loudly demands that Princeton go coeducational.

The other side of the coin, of course, is that the new Princetonians are much better students than their predecessors. They are more balanced and more experienced; they have better and more varied minds. They are highly motivated—even if they are not quite sure what they are after—and take pride in their performance. So serious are

they about their studies that one of the new medical problems is getting "clutched" at exam time, a kind of psychological panic ending in the infirmary. Ulcers are not unknown among the freshmen, and in a typical two-year span there were ten suicide attempts.

Some of the new intellectual climate can be attributed to the university itself, apart from its new admissions policies. There is the new curriculum, for example, which has got rid of the old freshman drill courses in dead languages and offers more variety of choice. Sociology and anthropology are not only taught now, but have their own departments. There are new courses in modern literature and modern art, which show the student the culture of our own time in the context of the past. Finally, the "area" programs in Africa, the Middle East, Russia, and the Far East let the undergraduate break completely out of the mold of prep-school courses.

Yet there is another side to the new model classroom. Among these students there are more boys who want to rise above their fathers and in a different field of work, seeking "ambitious" careers related to their college majors and their grades. This is vocationalism, job-hunting—and it is often accompanied by a philistine spirit. There is a

passion for grade-hunting, for beefing up the undergraduate transcript; graduate schools, too, are afflicted with an admissions scramble, and their deans pick their "freshmen" on grades. The engineering and science departments now have platoons of eager majors, some of whom are about as intellectual as longshoremen. The Geology Department has a smaller group of majors than it used to, with much higher averages; the old group of socialites looked on the subject as a gentlemanly pursuit, whereas these new boys are earnestly planning careers in oil and uranium.

The old Princeton had an air of late adolescence about it, of country club frivolity and unreality—what F. Scott Fitzgerald called "a meadow lark among the smokestacks." Now all is seriousness and purpose, perhaps too much so. Traditions, morality itself, must be changing when a generation chooses to regard stealing from the university store as amusing. Yet one Princeton tradition remains inviolate: the honor system. This seems the more remarkable at a time when grades are crucial for graduate-school acceptance and later careers, and when many students come from high schools where cheating is the unquestioned rule.

Raucus parties, such as the house-party caper opposite at the Quadrangle Club, are as old as Princeton. What would be hard to match today is the genteel gathering above, which includes future Supreme Court Justice John Marshall Harlan, '20, third from left, and Harvey S. Firestone, Jr., '20, right.

The principal results of a Princeton education today are two. The first is a self-conscious spirit of liberation, of a break with tradition, of a sense of belonging to *"our generation,"* exemplified in the cults of privacy, of subjectivism; students always use the phrases, "Of course, I'm prejudiced" or "in my judgment." Along with this goes a respect for differences and for individual behavior; minor eccentricity is a prized possession, to be cherished and, if necessary, contrived. The affectation of sloppy clothes, of beards, of behaving as unlike the Princeton stereotype as possible, is an outgrowth of this attitude. The old Princeton ideal is now called "a Princeton Charlie" or "a shallow tweed," and the clubs compete to recruit more exotic types. Most undergraduates are extremely critical of "college spirit" and solidarity and the sense of community. Interestingly enough, Yale is mentioned only in connection with football; all the talk is in relation to Harvard. Unlike Fitzgerald, who always worried whether he should have gone to New Haven, this generation wonders if it shouldn't have gone to Cambridge. Princeton today, in fact, resembles nothing quite so much as a rural Harvard, with overtones of an intellectual and anarchistic Dartmouth.

It is ironic to the older observer that the continual topic of conversation among these youthful oddballs and careful eccentrics is conformity. In a curious inversion of values, that pattern of "good" behavior once known as a sign of "character" and a product of "family," "tradition," and "breeding" is now labeled "conformity"—a syndrome to be feared, avoided, or at least disguised. For all that, they are intensely conservative, and it is doubtful whether many of their values are markedly changed by the college experience, however much their abilities may be sharpened. What the college does is merely to give them better techniques and more polished ways of defending the attitudes they came with (for whatever other reasons the alumni may fret about the new generation, on this they need not worry). They voted for Dewey and Eisenhower and Nixon (but not Goldwater); according to one liberal professor, "We switch them from Taft Republicans to Eisenhower Republicans. Anyone who tries to convert students is a fool." The one strong political conviction they do have is a firm commitment to the cause of civil rights.

If they are political conservatives, they are not political activists. They will not serve the Republican party,

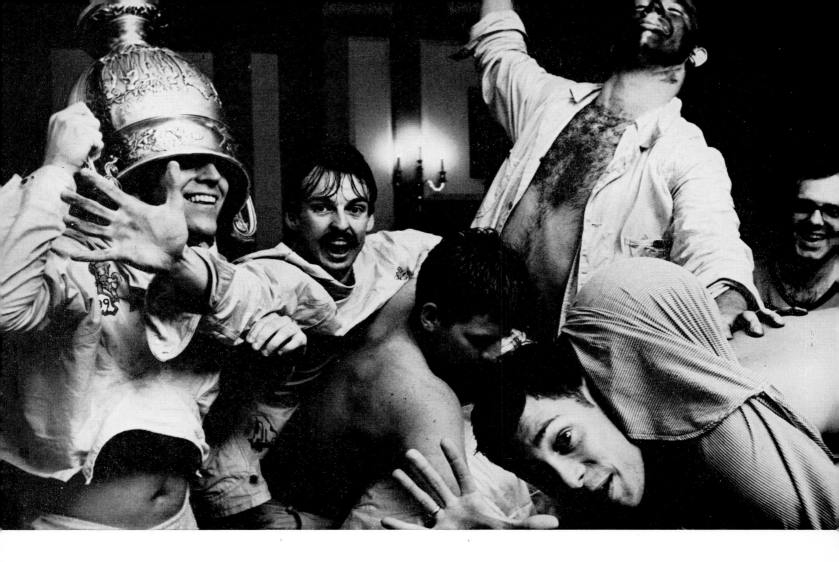

nor will they agitate. Here are no rebels against the predominant scheme of the welfare state. What they want is security, leisure, status, respect—but not money as such; they want only to rise above their middle-class backgrounds into the secure ranks of the diploma elite. In a time of general prosperity money means less than it used to, while the social elite is cracking and collapsing on all sides. Racial and religious discrimination has been shot through with so many exceptions in today's "society" that, in any effective sense, it is almost inoperative.

The surest sign of social change is the way in which the club system has been captured by this new generation, and now resembles the old only in the buildings. Indignant at the clubs' snobbish sorting out of sophomores, one of the first postwar classes signed a manifesto that no member would join a club unless the clubs offered a bid to every last man, and made the threat stick. Succeeding classes felt obligated to carry on this "100 per cent" pledge, and it has become the cardinal principle of the system.

The adjustment facing the clubs was formidable. Even in the old Princeton, which was composed almost entirely of "nice" upper-class Protestant boys, 20 per cent of a class still failed to meet club standards. Now the clubs were called upon to take *everyone*—this at a time when the social average had, in their view, declined catastrophically. Somehow, with every club taking a section as large as it can physically accommodate, each sophomore receives a bid somewhere. As a result, the social hierarchy has been shaken up so completely that the club stereotypes can hardly be said to exist any more, and individual club membership does not mean much. Colonial Club has risen to join Ivy, Cottage, Cap and Gown, and Tiger, and together they are known as "The Big Five"; the rest seem to follow in no particular order on a year-in, year-out basis. The clubs now compete for exotic types, with Koreans and Japanese currently the particular prizes. There are poets in Tiger Inn and theatrical directors in the Ivy Club. This last institution has been affected in a peculiar fashion by the new leveling spirit. In the old days it handed down invitations like Yale's Skull and Bones, whereas now only half of its invitees bother to show up, and not necessarily the most desirable half. Some years Ivy has had trouble in assembling a section because the "best" men in a class aren't interested in joining the club that Fitzgerald once described as "detached and breathlessly aristocratic"; to the new generation those are synonyms for dull and uninteresting.

One test of the system is its treatment of Jewish undergraduates. In the twenties only three or four might be taken into clubs each year. Semi-ostracism was not so much a problem that could be solved, or at least attacked, as it was a fact of life, accepted by Princeton clubs, American society, and possibly even by Jews themselves. But the present is very different. Anti-Semitism is no longer regarded as fashionable or even interesting, in fact is considered vulgar and "square." For a few years there was discussion of "the Jewish problem"; now there is none. It has been replaced by "the Negro problem." Will the clubs accept Negro members? Yes, it appears that they will, and do—not only American Negroes but the proud, haughty Africans.

Adding to the decline of interest in club life (one club, in fact, has folded) was the determination of the administration to do something about a group that has plagued the conscience of Princeton for generations—the "unclubbables," who would not or could not adapt themselves to the prevailing social standards of the campus. For them was constructed a "Quad" with an elaborate dining hall, lounge, library, and quarters for resident faculty members; the suites have built-in refrigerators and duplex living rooms. The undergraduate society which presides over these quarters, and organizes the social life of those boys who choose not to join eating clubs, cheerfully stages Greek plays, fiddles away at string quartets, plays three-dimensional chess, and throws faculty cocktail parties to its complete content.

This same spirit of indifference to the values of the old Princeton has spilled over into the realm of extracurricular activities. Woodrow Wilson thought the curse of college education was that the "side shows had taken over the main tent." In a peculiar, unplanned way, without a blow being struck by college authorities, the *mystique* of extracurricular activities fell under its own weight. Furthermore, and what is more important, it came about in a natural way, without compulsion from above, from the undergraduates themselves—or rather the new type of undergraduates Princeton selected.

Since 1946 the undergraduates, particularly the upperclassmen, have been spending a great deal more time and effort on their studies, and then quietly retiring to their clubs and squash courts to recharge their batteries for another assault on the library. The majority are not only apathetic to extracurricular activities but almost hostile to them; far from respecting the "activities" man, they sneer at him as a "do-gooder" or "campus politician." This shows itself in many ways. The chairman of the *Daily Princetonian*, once "Mr. Princeton," who carried the weight of the whole campus on his proud shoulders, now is an unknown, and writes his paper with the aid of a small clique. A "*Prince*" competition for editorial positions is now lucky to turn out ten fledgling journalists willing to make the effort. The Triangle Club, which once had three hundred sophomores trying out, is obliged to take freshmen. Since the seniors are too busy with their theses, the football manager is a junior now, and he presides over a small group of dedicated towel-carriers. Class offices and membership on the Undergraduate Council are reserved for, in the words of one administrator, "the not very bright"; one of the favorite jokes at the expense of the old system is to elect a complete nonentity class president on a farcical platform. Cheerleading, once a prestigious job handed down as a form of club patronage, is given to just about anybody willing. All publications exist on the brink of collapse, and the Whig-Clio debating society is an extinct volcano. For activist types, like zombies carrying on the traditions of a lost world, there is a favorite activity: hold a symposium, make a survey, write an editorial —on campus apathy.

The reasons for this misnamed "apathy" are understandable. First there are the increased demands of the curriculum. The work load, notoriously heavier than any other university's, has been increased. With no poor students and no "under-achievers," the competition is stiff and the level of expectation is high. To work, to study, has become a habit, almost a compulsion, and to let work slide is a danger; the *Princetonian* lost five chairmen in eight years to the academic axe. The new student simply has less time to spend on extracurricular activities.

More significant is the fact that he doesn't want to. He knew in secondary school that the university admissions office was not looking for brains alone but for boys who have participated in "all the best things of school life," and so to beef up his transcript of good grades he has dutifully gone out for the school paper or the Hi-Y or some such. When he arrives at college he is tired of all this enforced activity, and more than a little bored with it; now that he is safely admitted, the "fatigued freshman"—to use the phrase common among postwar college deans—can gratefully put aside childish things. He is frightened of the Princeton work load—and he is looking ahead to graduate school, whose admissions office is *not* looking for men who excel in "all the best things of school life" but those who excel in studies. So, except for a judicious membership at Princeton in the Pre-Law or Pre-Med Society—which takes little time and looks fine on a transcript—books are the first order of business.

Today's undergraduates put their steam into their studies and use their spare time for social life, which is regarded as pure diversion. There are more scheduled parties and many more girls around, even in the middle of the week. You work when you work and play when you play, in a sharp separation of intellectual life and social

An Open Letter to "Princeton Charlie"

In order to present the perspective of the current generation at Old Nassau, Horizon *asked Landon Y. Jones, '66, to comment on the views of Mr. Davies, for whom he worked during his undergraduate "meadow lark among the smokestacks." Mr. Jones recently joined the staff of Time Inc. in New York.*

No doubt Princeton has changed. An alumnus who graduated in the halcyon days before the war would feel uncomfortable returning to Princeton and facing the new generation. Few students would stop him on the walk to ask cheerfully the number of his class or the name of his club. No one would say hello. In fact, most students would rush by, probably on their way to find a seat in the jammed library or pick up a weekend date at the bus. I doubt whether they would regret the bruised feelings of the old gentleman, for to them he is a slightly amusing relic from a forgotten past. They think of him as a man floating through Princeton in an age when the green lawns were dotted with giddy preppies who washed down their intellectuality with gallons of frosty mint juleps; *his* idea of the present generation is dominated by a glimpse of a busy boy rushing down a shaded walk.

Princeton is not the gilded country club of the past, but four years there have taught me that it surely is not the brain factory that it must sometimes seem. For every student discussing Kant over a cup of coffee in the student center on Friday night, there are three more drinking beer and shooting pool with their dates in a club. I often think that the thing that has really changed at Princeton is the intensity of the student's life. In the twenties the boys could take it slow because Dad would always have a slot for them in the company. But the present Princeton students worked hard to get through the ivy gates and will have to work harder to "make good" in their careers; they unconsciously reflect the pressures of competition in both studies and parties.

In the social world of Princeton students, however, I found that the competition wears another mask. One must not be individually unique, but must somehow "fit in" and become known as a "good man." For example, Princeton is never so diverse as in the first week of the year when the wide-eyed freshmen make their initial rounds of the Gothic dorms. But as September fades into October, I have watched the four-star letter jackets and crew cuts of the high-school graduates blur into a more acceptable norm. At the same time, the prep-school graduates mothball their Harris tweeds and buy crinkly new pairs of blue jeans (well washed and bleached before being worn). The effect is contrived casualness; one often sees monogrammed shirts and seventy-dollar sport coats worn with a torn pair of corduroys. By assuming a mucker pose, the student implies that he could dress like a dandy if he wanted to.

One way to gather insights into the nature of college students is to keep an ear tuned to the campus jargon. Perhaps the most universal term I heard at Princeton was " 'cept," short for concept. It is used in describing phrases that condense much wisdom and can be amplified on exams. To say that "Protestantism grew from capitalism and the rise of the middle class" is a 'cept. One of the biggest 'cepts that students learn is to spot continuity in the midst of change. This 'cept applies aptly to Princeton. Change is evident any Saturday night when the prestigious eating clubs, former bastions of the grace and ease that characterized Princeton, are transformed into raucous dens of tee-shirted young men wallowing through puddles of spilled beer. I remember standing in a club watching some friends pour beer on each other and then looking up wonderingly at the framed portraits of the dignified founding members of the club.

To understand today's Princeton, we must look beneath this relaxation of social standards and find the real continuity with the past. The link is idealism—for I have found that Princeton students share a common idealism about their ability to make constructive use of their lives in a tangled world. It is not the sort of rebellious idealism that one finds at Berkeley; it is more the belief that society can be changed from the inside. Princeton students are not rebels; they will slip into three-piece suits after graduation as easily as they slipped into denim shirts and jeans when coming to Princeton. They lean toward a universal medium. I find that most of my friends wanted the respect of their peers more than anything else. They hope to find "meaningful" occupations in which the constructive values and rewards of their work will be primary and money will be but a by-product of virtue.

Talking to seniors during the graduation ceremonies, I realized that the vast majority of them felt that they had received the finest education in the world. They also felt that they had learned the social graces that would serve them well in later life. Like every generation, they were convinced that they were graduating into a chaotic world, and that if their fathers were shocked by the attitudes of their sons, they had better learn that the old answers would no longer serve.

These students see life in terms of a great game—you have to play the rules. They played the game right and got into Princeton; if they keep on playing the game right, they will become successes. That is why a man like Jack Kennedy could capture the imagination of the college generation: he played the game according to the rules, was not afraid of new approaches, and did it all with such casual style. So the old gentleman who is shocked by the rudeness of the Princeton students will have to nurse his wound without sympathy, for these are students who have no time for the past.

life. If, on the one hand, this ruptures the Wilsonian seamless web of "the consciousness of work" in the midst of play and long walks in the woods with your teacher, at the same time this is how graduate students and even professors live—an adult pattern of behavior and therefore a preparation for real life. One of the peculiar sights amidst the squalor of dormitory rooms is the ubiquitous TV set, located in the paneled fireplace; one of the favorite "social" activities is what undergraduates call "watching tube," hours and hours of horse operas and late late shows, with beer can in hand—just like grownups.

Another aspect of this changing emphasis is irreverence toward campus traditions. Senior singing from the steps of Nassau Hall was born in 1760 and died out a hundred and ninety years later. Clapper stealing necessarily ended when the instrument was welded to the bell. Freshmen don't wear black skullcaps any more, and since they don't wear ties, they don't wear black ties. Freshmen and sophomores eat in commons side by side in undifferentiated togetherness, unaware of one another's identity—they can only guess who is in their class.

This spirit of indifference has even grasped the tail of the oldest sacred cow of them all, college athletics. Athletes take books along on trips and use the "enemy's" library; according to one coach, just as they are better students as seniors than they are as sophomores, the seniors on the team are worse athletes than they were in their sophomore year. The teams, even within the gentle confines of the once mighty Ivy League, generally do not do very well. The squads are small, because students will not go out for a sport only to sit on the bench and be mincemeat for the varsity; the common philosophy is, "Either I play on the varsity or I quit." Hockey, the prep-school sport, is way down for obvious reasons; one freshman class had only twenty-two skaters in it, another didn't have any goalie at all. Lacrosse, played by the fashionable Maryland set, has slumped in inverse proportion to the steady rise in admissions standards. Track is in indifferent shape, the crew does not win, and baseball is semi-farcical, with errors in astronomical numbers. Basketball, on the other hand, has found some high-school giants—the most notable being the legendary Bill Bradley —and has done much better.

Fortunately, nobody really cares about the records of the teams; it was not by accident that the new gymnasium has a smaller trophy room than the old. Sport is regarded as a private thing, pursued for pleasure and exercise, to be carried on after college. Tennis is the most popular sport and the number of courts has had to be increased, along with the number of squash courts. Athletic authorities have been dumbfounded by the requests for handball facilities, a game previously restricted to policemen.

For a while the one exception to all this was football,

an affair entirely too serious for the university to allow the new climate to chill. After Bill Roper retired in 1930, and his successor produced a disastrous season, Princeton took a realistic look at football and hired a "big time," full-time coach, Fritz Crisler, from the midwest, where "spring" practice started on February 15. Soon Princeton was winning again. But after the war, following a series of embarrassing defeats at the hands of their former sectional rivals—Navy crushed Princeton once by a score of 65 to 7—the Ivy League presidents decided to get out of the big time. They would form a league of their own. To dramatize their purity they somewhat illogically abolished spring practice, although permitting it in other sports, and they refused to play any team that did practice in the spring—ensuring thereby that they would never have to play any really good teams.

Understandably, the game is no longer of great interest to the new undergraduates. In place of the old pregame anxiety, there is only indifference, without cheers, singing, and pep meetings. The competition for the football managership, once a strenuous contest to be a valet for these golden heroes, is sparsely attended, and cheerleaders are hard to find. To the students the fall is simply a series of cheerful social weekends. In one stretch Princeton beat Yale six years in a row, without any special elation on the one side or despondency on the other. The steel goal posts are now embedded in concrete, but there really is no need; this crowd wouldn't knock over a waxworks and has never seen a snake dance.

The public, likewise, is not much interested in Ivy football, preferring the professional Sunday brand; the Pennsylvania Railroad yards in Princeton, which used to hold as many as twenty special trains at big games, are now torn up. Only the alumni are still enthusiastic, concerned about the Princeton record, and predictably mutinous opponents of the bans on spring practice and subsidization.

It is now the habit of sports writers to hail the Ivy League as a citadel of purity, and so it is, compared with the scandals that have rocked intercollegiate football elsewhere. But football still pays a large percentage of the college's fixed athletic costs. And football also gives Princeton's alumni something to watch, a return for the very considerable financial sacrifices they are expected to make. It's just about the only contact they have left, after all, with the Princeton they knew as undergraduates.

John Davies, '41, whose raccoon coat and mittens have become a nostalgic fixture at football games in Palmer Stadium, is editor of the Princeton University Alumni Weekly. *This article was adapted from his forthcoming history of his alma mater,* Tiger in the Ivy: The Princeton Man and his University, 1900-1967, *which will be published in February by Devin-Adair Company.*

"Work when you work, play when you play" is the credo of these students carousing around the water sculpture in front of the new Woodrow Wilson Institute.

HABITAT 67

A young architect
designs a living place
for the future
at the Montreal Fair

By DAVID JACOBS

R. Buckminster Fuller and Moshe Safdie have revolutionary ideas about what ought to be done with the present and future city. Although the physical characteristics of their architecture are dissimilar, they approach their art with much the same vocabulary. Both are inclined to relate urban development to organic phenomena; both are committed to economical construction; both place great emphasis on the creation of a total environment and therefore regard the individual building as subservient to the whole urban structure. Fuller's whole is an inclusive dome and Safdie's, a staggered, diffusive assemblage of like units.

Safdie, a twenty-eight-year-old architect, was born at a much better time for urban architects than was Fuller (now seventy-one), who began to envision tomorrow's cities before anyone had complaints about today's. When he was in his twenties, Fuller developed a prefabricated, motorized "Dymaxion" (for dynamic and maximum efficiency) house, and in 1928 offered the patent to the American Institute of Architects. Not only did that organization refuse to accept it, but it passed a resolution condemning the whole concept of prefabrication. But Fuller persisted, shrugging off the crackpot label, financing his own projects when he could, designing houses, buses, cars, and anything else designable. After World War II he perfected his "geodesic" dome, the all-purpose enclosure for army barracks, concert halls, baseball parks, and even, Fuller insists, for whole cities.

Meanwhile, the city has been overtaken by all the problems that Fuller anticipated many years ago. Thanks to his persistence, almost any scheme to improve the city is welcomed, and a young man like Safdie, who was born in Israel in 1938 and received his architectural degree from McGill University in 1961, will not have to spend years in his prime, screaming just to be heard.

The work of both men will be on display at Expo 67, the international exhibition that will open this April in Montreal. Fuller describes his United States Pavilion as "a prototype 'environmental valve' which will enclose sufficient space for whole communities to live in benign physical microcosm." Safdie's Habitat 67, a housing development, is presented by Expo simply as "an exhibition of modern architecture." Though both are revolutionary

in terms of their implication for the future of urban housing, Habitat belongs equally to the here and now; it works within the framework of the existing city. People will, in fact, soon be moving in.

Habitat is mass-produced, prefabricated housing, manufactured in a plant on the site. The assembly procedure is simple. A reinforced concrete box, measuring thirty-eight and a half feet in length, seventeen and a half in width, and ten in height, is the basic unit; various combinations of the box form houses of four to eight rooms. After the concrete is poured into the mold inside the plant, the box is rolled outside to dry. Then the concrete is sandblasted, floors are laid, windows inserted, kitchens installed, and the bathrooms, precast of two pieces of plastic, are dropped in. Finally a crane lifts the box into place and workmen quickly secure it. Stacked to a height of 120 feet, on a tract 950 by 300 feet, the dwellings are surprisingly different from one another in size and layout.

The relative absence from architectural history of the stepped block-upon-block structure suggests what a complex form this seemingly simple concept really is. The few stepped boxes that do come to mind—the Pueblo apartment complexes, for example—were generally built into the sides of elevations or depressions; thus they were not so much stacked as secured into vertical foundations. One of the greatest attractions of stepping is that it exposes so many planes to light and air. To accomplish this the entire complex must include almost as many cavities as solid sections. The structure generates not only the downward

Habitat's building blocks, opposite, are stacked up to present an intricate array of light and shade, mass and void. In contrast, R. Buckminster Fuller's model city, below, is set apart and encompassed by a simple geodesic dome.

Mounted on tracks, at left, a giant crane sets finished components into the proper slots in Moshe Safdie's 13-story structure. Above, Safdie makes one of his frequent visits to the building which, when completed, will zigzag along 950 feet of waterfront. The individual units, as shown in the model at right, are joined by broad pedestrian walks.

thrust of post-and-lintel architecture but an outward thrust similar to that of a vaulted cathedral. Since most block-units rest on two or more other units and frequently roof an open area, the tendency is for the supporters to fall outward under the weight of the supported. Now, even if we assume that the boxes are so stacked that perfect balance minimizes outward thrust—which, by the way, they are—we are still left with the ground-level, corner units, which must endure the entire weight of the complex. The observant child, building with wooden blocks, knows that these units are usually the first to collapse (because they slide out from under the complex—a perfect example of thrust).

With Habitat Safdie demonstrates that the functional elements of a staggered complex, such as elevator shafts and pedestrian walkways, can be used to support and strengthen the structure. He has placed the elevator shafts at points of stress, so that as the pressure from the thrust is transferred downward and outward from the topmost unit, the shaft absorbs the thrust and reroutes it straight down to the ground. Pedestrian walkways lace together the various units and levels of Habitat. The walkways, which are strung with steel cables, provide Habitat with the same shock-absorbing elasticity that a suspension bridge has under stress.

Habitat's most significant implication for the future of urban housing lies in the fact that it neither asks the city resident to readjust his life to suit the architecture nor asks the city to level itself to make room for the revolution. For many years the town house was the ideal urban dwelling, but when the economics of the city made individual houses wasteful and impractical, the multiple-family dwelling prevailed. For the most part apartment houses have been adapted from conventional building forms. The high-rise apartment house is simply a small skyscraper. The garden apartment or apartment development, such as New York's Stuyvesant Town, which turns its back on the surrounding city, is a variation of the old Garden City idea, which was always intended for suburbs. Planned towns like Reston, Virginia, and Columbia, Maryland, are also designed for suburbs, although they probably would enhance a city; but here the problem is that at least a thousand bare, uninhabitated acres would be needed, and no northern American city is prepared to raze that much land. Habitat, however, can be built on a rambling tract, *over* essential streets if necessary, *around* buildings or building complexes. Living in one of its houses will be much like living in a town house, but because the units are stacked, the complex will constitute high-density housing, capable of competing economically with skyscraper dwellings. It is perfectly conceivable, then, that a Habitat could creep up on a city, curing blight without affecting the character of the city.

Habitat is at once massive and airy, colossal yet approachable. Parking is distributed along the ground level (thus avoiding the need for lots) under the structure.

From his parking space the resident takes an elevator or steps (which are snow-melting) to his level, and walks to his house. The staggered structure provides protection while the homebound resident is outdoors, yet the architect has considered the one man who might enjoy walking in the rain: most of the streets are partially covered and partially exposed. Many of the houses have two stories with a terrace on each, so that while the resident sits outside having his cocktail, he can watch his children playing on the terrace below. Regarding privacy as sacred, Safdie has alternated the positions of the gardened terraces—one faces north, a neighbor's south, et cetera—thus concealing good-sized portions of each terrace from neighborly eyes. One has a splendid view of the harbor and downtown Montreal. Inside, the houses are roomy and well laid out. Although they are not radically different from the dwellings in a very good contemporary housing development, they are lighter than most—and quieter. There is nothing intimidating about Habitat and nothing sterile.

The flaw in Habitat is that there is not enough of it, and the nature of the project makes this a very grave flaw indeed. When he designed the project as his undergraduate thesis at McGill, Safdie planned a thousand dwellings, but the Habitat that is going up contains only one hundred and fifty-eight. As the architect admits, even a thousand units would not be profitable because the project is a prototype; but a large complex would at least contain enough families to make a diverse urban community, able to support traditional community functions. Research, experimentation, the dies for the bathrooms, the concrete molds, the specially engineered dollies and cranes, were all expensive, and their cost will have to be distributed among a hundred and fifty-eight units instead of a thousand. As a result Habitat will not be the economical structure that it could have been, and the concept of the structure as a whole community will have to be proved some other time.

Still, Expo 67 deserves credit for sticking its neck out at all. Habitat is costing eleven and a half million dollars and will be sold at a loss when the exhibition closes. Having decided to spend that much on a housing project, the officials must have been tempted to hire a "name," but they accepted instead the proposal of an unknown architect. Habitat is Safdie's first major commission, and one that he can expect to see imitated.

Although the people in charge of Expo decided to do without an official symbol, many have been calling Habitat the exposition symbol—in much the same way that Parisians, in 1889, insisted upon considering the Eiffel Tower as the symbol of the Paris Exposition. It seemed, somehow, to characterize their age. Apparently, today, what we would most like to have symbolize our age is a place to live.

David Jacobs is currently at work on two books—one of them, A Place to Live, *concerned with urban housing.*

One of the greatest admirers of his own haunting portraits was the eccentric Russian called John Graham

In the case of the late John Graham, even more than with most painters, it is difficult to separate the artist from his art; in fact, there are those who believe that he deliberately tried to shape his life—or at least his legend—into a conscious work of art that would demonstrate his concept of "hermetically sealed purity."

Graham was one of those true exotics that periodically flash through an epoch, calling attention to themselves by their very strangeness. Born in Russia in 1881 of an aristocratic family named Dabrowsky, he studied law before accepting a commission in the Czar's cavalry. As an aide-de-camp to Emperor Nicholas II (portraits of three Nicholases—the Czar, the saint, and Lenin—were kept beside his bed the rest of his life), he thrice received the St. George Cross. Arrested and condemned to death by the Bolsheviks, he later claimed that one of his captors arranged his escape to Paris after being impressed by his artistic talent.

Sometime in the twenties he arrived in this country, took Graham as his name, married an American, and was naturalized—although to the end he remained very much the cosmopolitan Russian aristocrat in exile. After studying with John Sloan at the Art Students League, Graham soon began to function as a link between the Parisian avant-garde he had come to know and promising American artists like Gorky, De Kooning, Pollock, and David Smith. As Thomas B. Hess of *Art News* has explained it, "Graham brought to the New York 'provinces' a sophistication and original turn of mind that was sadly missing from the scene."

The gift was reciprocal: from his associates, particularly De Kooning, he borrowed elements of style and treatment for his own painting, eventually attaining—since Graham seldom exhibited anything—a substantial underground reputation.

By the 1940's, however, he had renounced modernism and denounced Picasso, who, he decided, was "grinding out merchandise." Knowledge is the

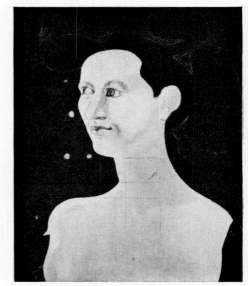

KALI YUGA, OIL, 1950

only approach to the divinity of art, he wrote in a mystical monograph published posthumously: "This heroic task is not for the feeble-minded, soft, scheming, petti-foggers, double-dealers, and scavengers."

For himself, Graham turned back to the classicists for inspiration, artists like Leonardo, Raphael, Cellini, Donatello, and Ingres. "I'm maybe not as good as Raphael," he once conceded, "but there is more tension in my canvases." The result is a small but haunting group of paintings and oil drawings, their intensity heightened by figures in majestic poses, elegant draftsmanship, and an unorthodox use of color (see opposite). He also frequently embellished his pictures with astro-symbols and calligraphy (left), usually in Greek (he was said to be fluent in twelve languages). His later portraits, of enigmatic beauties with "one wandering eye" (above), were often disfigured with slashed necks and wrists ("Human blood," he wrote, "is beauty integral").

This compact, mysterious body of work, as seen at a recent New York exhibition, offers ample proof that Graham should be taken seriously, if not necessarily at his own estimate. "I think perhaps," he confided shortly before his death in 1961, "that I am probably the best painter in the world."

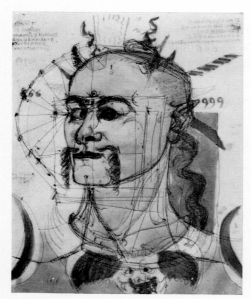

SELF-PORTRAIT, OIL DRAWING

SELF-PORTRAIT, OIL, 1944

I-beams and steel rods turn into sculpture under the welding torch of Anthony Caro

Anthony Caro's abstract sculpture is equally at rest in the Tate Gallery (right) or in nature. His 1961 piece, Sculpture 1 *(above), adds its own tension to a London back yard, while* Prospect *(below) blends into the campus of Bennington College.*

PHOTOGRAPHS ANDRE EMMERICH GALLERY, N.Y.

The central fact about the so-called "minimal" or "ABC" sculpture that currently dominates the scene is its concentrated anonymity. So impersonalized are the products of its most polished practitioners—such as Anthony Caro, a 42-year-old British engineer-turned-artist—that the hand of the sculptor is nowhere apparent. Instead, Caro and his fellow neo-Constructivists prefer to arrange the functional materials of an

EARLY ONE MORNING, 1962

industrial age into spare, impersonal forms, making, in the view of one critic, "cool and plain statements of self-sufficiency."

Needless to say, the advent of these "primary structures"—to use still another term for them—has unleashed almost as many different critical reactions as there are angles from which to view them. Hilton Kramer of *The New York Times,* for instance, concluded

that "a new aesthetic era is upon us," to which *Time* magazine responded by describing Caro's sculpture as "an explosion in a boiler factory." Barbara Rose, writing in *Art in America,* even addresses part of her essay to the numerous complaints about the neutrality of minimal art: "Boring the public is one way of testing its commitment."

All discussions of ABC sculpture must eventually touch on the works of Caro,

the former apprentice of Henry Moore and the man who, in 1960, discovered that "you didn't need to make a sculpture of somebody crying in order to make a sculpture cry." A measure of his success came last summer when his redcoated *Early One Morning* (above), a melange of I-beams and steel rods, was exhibited in the British Pavilion at the Venice Biennale; he was the only British sculptor so honored.

Red Grooms lost his loft but not until he had preserved the studio and all his friends in this scale model

Two friends in close-up: Elise Suttman (above), who is on the couch, and Candis Brown (opposite), behind the partition.

LOFT ON 26TH STREET, 1965

R ed Grooms is an expressionist painter with Pop tendencies, a talented eclectic, and an unabashed sentimentalist. Months before he was evicted from his Manhattan loft studio, he had determined to memorialize it. "When the luncheonette on the ground floor burned the summer of 1964," he remembers, "we knew our days in the loft were numbered. So I started building a scale replica of the place." The model, appropriately entitled *Loft on 26th Street*, measures 30 by 35 by 70 inches and is made of plywood, cardboard, and styrofoam, all coated with acrylic paint. The cardboard cutouts are friends of the artist (far right) and his wife Mimi (leaning on chair, center).

Grooms exercised the same painstaking care ("Some of the portraits took fourteen hours to paint") and comic touch in 1963 when he made a three-dimensional collage of the famous banquet Picasso staged for Henri Rousseau. "I can't remember now how I got started on stick-out constructions," says Grooms, "unless it was a natural progression from my early textural experiments with cardboard on canvas and then building sets for 'happenings' and movies." For the past three years Grooms has been producing his own avant-garde motion pictures under the imprimatur of Ruckus Films.

Back to Bachimba

A hyphenated American discovers that he can't go home again

I am a *pocho* from Bachimba, a rather small Mexican village in the state of Chihuahua, where my father fought with the army of Pancho Villa. He was, in fact, the only private in Villa's army.

Pocho is ordinarily a derogatory term in Mexico (to define it succinctly, a *pocho* is a Mexican slob who has pretensions of being a gringo sonofabitch), but I use it in a very special sense. To me that word has come to mean "uprooted Mexican," and that's what I have been all my life. Though my entire upbringing and education took place in the United States, I have never felt completely American; and when I am in Mexico, I sometimes feel like a displaced gringo with a curiously Mexican name—Enrique Preciliano Lopez y Martinez de Sepulveda de Sapien (. . . de Quien-sabe-quien). One might conclude that I'm either a schizo-cultural Mexican or a cultured schizoid American.

In any event, the schizo-ing began a long time ago, when my father and many of Pancho Villa's troops fled across the border to escape the oncoming *federales* who eventually defeated Villa. My mother and I, traveling across the hot desert plains in a buckboard wagon, joined my father in El Paso, Texas, a few days after his hurried departure. With more and more Villistas swarming into El Paso every day, it was quickly apparent that jobs would be exceedingly scarce and insecure; so my parents packed our few belongings and we took the first available bus to Denver. My father had hoped to move to Chicago because the name sounded so Mexican, but my mother's meager savings were hardly enough to buy tickets for Colorado.

There we moved into a ghetto of Spanish-speaking residents who chose to call themselves Spanish-Americans and resented the sudden migration of their brethren from Mexico, whom they sneeringly called *surumatos* (slang for "southerners"). These so-called Spanish-Americans claimed direct descent from the original conquistadores of Spain. They also insisted that they had *never* been Mexicans, since their region of New Spain (later annexed to the United States) was never a part of Mexico. But what they claimed most vociferously—and erroneously— was an absence of Indian ancestry. It made no difference that any objective observer could see by merely looking at them the results of considerable fraternization between the conquering Spaniards and the Comanche and Navaho women who crossed their paths. Still, these *manitos*, as they were snidely labeled by the *surumatos*, stubbornly refused to be identified with Mexico, and would actually fight anyone who called them Mexican. So intense was this intergroup rivalry that the bitterest "race riots" I have ever witnessed—and engaged in—were between the look-alike, talk-alike *surumatos* and *manitos* who lived near Denver's Curtis Park. In retrospect the harsh conflicts between us were all the more silly and self-defeating when one recalls that we were all lumped together as "spiks" and "greasers" by the Anglo-Saxon community.

Predictably enough, we *surumatos* began huddling together in a subneighborhood within the larger ghetto, and it was there that I became painfully aware that my father had been the only private in Pancho Villa's army. Most of my friends were the sons of captains, colonels, majors, and even generals, though a few fathers were admittedly mere sergeants and corporals. My father alone had been a lowly private in that famous Division del Norte. Natu-

By ENRIQUE HANK LOPEZ

rally I developed a most painful complex, which led me to all sorts of compensatory fibs. During one brief spell I fancied my father as a member of the dreaded *los dorados*, the "golden ones," who were Villa's favorite henchmen. (Later I was to learn that my father's cousin, Martin Lopez, was a genuine and quite notorious *dorado*.) But all my inventions were quickly un-invented by my very own father, who seemed to take a perverse delight in being Pancho's only private.

No doubt my chagrin was accentuated by the fact that Pancho Villa's exploits were a constant topic of conversation in our household. My entire childhood seems to be shadowed by his presence. At our dinner table, almost every night, we would listen to endlessly repeated accounts of this battle, that stratagem, or some great act of Robin Hood kindness by *el centauro del norte*. I remember how angry my parents were when they saw Wallace Beery in *Viva Villa!* "Garbage by stupid gringos" they called it. They were particularly offended by the sweaty, unshaven sloppiness of Beery's portrayal. "Pancho Villa was clean and orderly, no matter how much he chased after women. This man's a dirty swine."

As if to deepen our sense of *Villismo*, my parents also taught us "Adelita" and "*Se llevaron el cañon para Bachimba*" ("They took the cannons to Bachimba"), the two most famous songs of the Mexican revolution. Some twenty years later (during my stint at Harvard Law School), while strolling along the Charles River, I would find myself softly singing "*Se llevaron el cañon para Bachimba, para Bachimba, para Bachimba*" over and over again. That's all I could remember of that poignant rebel song. Though I had been born there, I had always regarded "Bachimba" as a fictitious, made-up, Lewis Carroll kind of word. So that eight years ago, when I first returned to Mexico, I was literally stunned when I came to a crossroad south of Chihuahua and saw an old road marker: "Bachimba 18 km." Then it really exists—I shouted inwardly—Bachimba is a real town! Swinging onto the narrow, poorly paved road, I gunned the motor and sped toward the town I'd been singing about since infancy. It turned out to be a quiet, dusty village with a bleak worn-down plaza that was surrounded by nondescript buildings of uncertain vintage.

Aside from the songs about Bachimba and Adelita and all the folk tales about Villa's guerrilla fighters, my early years were strongly influenced by our neighborhood celebrations of Mexico's two most important patriotic events: Mexican Independence Day on September 16, and the anniversary of the battle of Puebla on May 5. On those two dates Mexicans all over the world are likely to become extremely chauvinistic. In Denver we would stage annual parades that included three or four floats skimpily decorated with crepe-paper streamers, a small band, several adults in threadbare battle dress, and hundreds of kids marching in wild disorder. It was during one of these parades—I was ten years old then—that I was seized with acute appendicitis and had to be rushed to a hospital. The doctor subsequently told my mother that I had made a long, impassioned speech about the early revolutionist Miguel Hidalgo while the anesthetic was taking hold, and she explained with pardonable pride that it was the speech I was to make at Turner Hall that evening. Mine was one of the twenty-three *discursos* scheduled on the postparade program, a copy of which my mother still retains. My only regret was missing the annual *discurso* of Don Miguel Gomez, my godfather, a deep-throated orator who would always climax his speech by falling to his knees and dramatically kissing the floor, almost weeping as he loudly proclaimed: "*Ay, Mexico! Beso tu tierra, tu mero corazón*" ("Ah, Mexico! I kiss your sacred soil, the very heart of you"). He gave the same oration for seventeen years, word for word and gesture for gesture, and it never failed to bring tears to his eyes. But not once did he return to Chihuahua, even for a brief visit.

My personal Mexican-ness eventually produced serious problems for me. Upon entering grade school I learned English rapidly and rather well, always ranking either first or second in my class; yet the hard core of me remained stubbornly Mexican. This chauvinism may have been a reaction to the constant racial prejudice we encountered on all sides. The neighborhood cops were always running us off the streets and calling us "dirty greasers," and most of our teachers frankly regarded us as totally inferior. I still remember the galling disdain of my sixth-grade teacher, whose constant mimicking of our heavily accented speech drove me to a desperate study of *Webster's Dictionary* in the hope of acquiring a vocabulary larger than hers. Sadly enough, I succeeded only too well, and for the next few years I spoke the most ridiculous high-flown rhetoric in the Denver public schools. One of my favorite words was "indubitably," and it must have driven everyone mad. I finally got rid of my accent by constantly reciting "Peter Piper picked a peck of pickled peppers" with little round pebbles in my mouth. Somewhere I had read about Demosthenes.

During this phase of my childhood the cultural tug of war known as "Americanization" almost pulled me apart. There were moments when I would identify completely with the gringo world (what could have been more American than my earnest high-voiced portrayal of George Washington, however ridiculous the cotton wig my mother had fashioned for me?); then quite suddenly I would feel so acutely Mexican that I would stammer over the simplest English phrase. I was so ready to take offense at the slightest slur against Mexicans that I would imagine prejudice where none existed. But on other occasions, in full confidence of my belonging, I would venture forth into social areas that I should have realized were clearly forbidden to little *chicanos* from Curtis Park. The inevitable rebuffs would leave me floundering in self-pity; it was small comfort to know that other minority groups suffered even worse rebuffs than we did.

The only non-Mexican boy on our street was a Negro named Leroy Logan, who was probably my closest childhood friend. Leroy was the best athlete, the best whistler, the best liar, the best horseshoe player, the best marble shooter, the best mumblety-pegger, and the best shoplifter in our neighborhood. He was also my "partner," and I thus entitled myself to a fifty-fifty share of all his large triumphs and petty thefts. Because he considered "Mexican" a derogatory word bordering on obscenity, Leroy would pronounce it "Mesican" so as to soften its harshness. But once in a while, when he'd get angry with me, he would call me a "lousy Mesican greasy spik" with the most extraordinarily effective hissing one can imagine. And I'm embarrassed to admit that I would retaliate by calling him "alligator bait." As a matter of fact, just after I had returned from the hospital, he came to visit me, and I thoughtlessly greeted him with a flippant "Hi, alligator ba——" I never finished the phrase because Leroy whacked me on the stomach with a Ping-pong paddle and rushed out of my house with great, sobbing anger.

Weeks later, when we had re-established a rather cool rapport, I tried to make up for my stupid insult by helping him steal cabbages from the vegetable trucks that rumbled through our neighborhood on their way to the produce markets. They would come down Larimer Street in the early dawn, and Leroy and I would sneak up behind them at the 27th Street stop sign, where they were forced to pause for cross traffic. Then Leroy, with a hooked pole he had invented, would stab the top cabbages and roll them off the truck. I would be waiting below to catch them with an open gunny sack. Our system was fabulously successful for a while, and we found a ready market for the stolen goods; but one morning, as I started to unfurl my sack, a fairly large cabbage conked me on the head. Screaming with pain, I lunged at Leroy and tried to bite him. He, laughing all the while—it was obviously a funny scene—glided out of my reach, and finally ran into a nearby alley. We never engaged in commercial affairs thereafter.

Still and all, I remember him with great affection and a touch of sadness. I say sadness because eventually Leroy was to suffer the misery of being an outsider in an already outside ghetto. As he grew older, it was apparent that he longed to be a Mexican, that he felt terribly dark and alone. "Sometimes," he would tell me, "I feel like my damn skin's too tight, like I'm gonna bust out of it." One cold February night I found him in the coal shed behind Pacheco's store, desperately scraping his forearm with sandpaper, the hurt tears streaming down his face. "I got to get this off, man. I can't stand all this blackness." We stood there quietly staring at the floor for a long, anguished moment, both of us miserable beyond word or gesture. Finally he drew a deep breath, blew his nose loudly, and mumbled half audibly, "Man, you sure lucky to be a Mesican."

Not long after this incident Leroy moved out of Denver to live with relatives in Georgia. When I saw him off at the bus station, he grabbed my shoulder and whispered huskily, "You gonna miss me, man. You watch what I tellya." "Indubitably," I said. "Aw, man, cut that stuff. You the most fancy-pants Mesican I know." Those were his last words to me, and they caused a considerable dent in my ego. Not enough, however, to diminish my penchant for fancy language. The dictionary continued to be my comic book well into high school.

Speaking of language, I am reminded of a most peculiar circumstance: almost every Mexican-American lawyer that I've ever met speaks English with a noticeable Spanish accent, this despite the fact that they have all been born, reared, and educated exclusively in America. Of the forty-eight lawyers I have in mind, only three of us are free of any accent. Needless to say our "cultural drag" has been weighty and persistent. And one must presume that our ethnic hyphens shall be with us for many years to come.

My own Mexican-ness, after years of decline at Harvard University, suddenly burst forth again when I returned to Chihuahua and stumbled on the town of Bachimba. I had long conversations with an uncle I'd never met before, my father's younger brother, Ramon. It was Tio Ramon who chilled my spine with eyewitness stories about Pancho Villa's legendary *dorados*, one of whom was Martin Lopez. "He was your second cousin. The bravest young buck in Villa's army. And he became a *dorado* when he was scarcely seventeen years old because he dared to defy Pancho Villa himself. As your papa may have told you, Villa had a bad habit of burying treasure up in the mountains and also burying the man he took with him to dig the hole for it. Well, one day he chose Martin Lopez to go with him. Deep in the mountains they went, near Parral. And when they got to a suitably lonely place, Pancho Villa told him to dig a hole with pick and shovel. Then, when Martin had dug down to his waist, Villa leveled a gun at the boy. "Say your prayers, *muchacho*. You shall stay here with the gold— forever." But Martin had come prepared. In his large right boot he had a gun, and when he rose from his bent position, he was pointing that gun at Villa. They stood there, both ready to fire, for several seconds, and finally Don Pancho started to laugh in that wonderful way of his. "*Bravo, bravo, muchacho!* You've got more guts than a man. Get out of that hole, boy. I need you for my *dorados.*"

Tio Ramon's eyes were wet with pride. "But what is more important, he died with great valor. Two years later, after he had terrorized the *federales* and Pershing's gringo soldiers, he was finally wounded and captured here in Bachimba. It was a bad wound in his leg, finally turning to gangrene. Then one Sunday morning they hauled Martin Lopez and three other prisoners to the plaza. One by one they executed the three lesser prisoners against that wall. I was up on the church tower watching it all. Finally it was your uncle's turn. They dragged him off the buckboard wagon and handed him his crutches. Slowly, painfully, he hobbled to the wall and stood there. Very straight he stood. 'Do you have any last words?' said the captain of the firing squad. With great pride Martin tossed his crutches aside and stood very tall on his one good leg. 'Give me, you yellow bastards, give me a gun—and I'll show you who is the man among . . .' Eight bullets crashed into his chest and face, and I never heard that final word. That was your second cousin. You would have been proud to know him."

As I listened to Tio Ramon's soft nostalgic voice that evening, there in the sputtering light of the kerosene lamp on his back patio, I felt as intensely Mexican as I shall ever feel.

But not for long. Within six weeks I was destined to feel *less* Mexican than I had ever felt. The scene of my trauma was the Centro Mexicano de Escritores, where the finest young writers of Mexico met regularly to discuss works in progress and to engage in erudite literary and philosophical discussions. Week after week I sat among them, dumb struck by my inadequacy in Spanish and my total ignorance of their whole frame of reference. How could I have possibly imagined that I was Mexican? Those conversations were a dense tangle of local and private allusions, and the few threads I could grasp only magnified my ignorance. The novelist Juan Rulfo was then reading the initial drafts of his *Pedro Páramo*, later to be acclaimed the best avant-garde fiction in Mexican literature. Now that I have soaked myself in the *ambiance* of Mexico, Rulfo's novel intrigues me beyond measure; but when he first read it at the Centro, he might just as well have been reading "Jabberwocky" in Swahili for all I understood of it. And because all of the other Mexican writers knew and greatly appreciated *Páramo,* I could only assume that I was really "too gringo" to comprehend it. For this reason, I, a person with no great talent for reticence, never opened my mouth at the Centro. In fact, I was so shell-shocked by those sessions that I even found it difficult to converse with my housekeeper about such simple matters as dirty laundry or the loose doorknob in the bathroom.

Can any of us really go home again? I, for one, am convinced that I have no true home, that I must reconcile myself to a schizo-cultural limbo, with a mere hyphen to provide some slight cohesion between my split selves. This inevitable splitting is a plague and a pleasure. Some mornings as I glide down the Paseo de la Reforma, perhaps the most beautiful boulevard in the world, I am suddenly angered by the *machismo,* or aggressive maleness, of Mexican drivers who crowd and bully their screeching machines through dense traffic. What terrible insecurity, what awful dread of emasculation, produces such assertive bully-boy conduct behind a steering wheel? Whatever the reasons, there is a part of me that can never accept this much-celebrated *machismo.* Nor can I accept the exaggerated nationalism one so frequently encounters in the press, on movie screens, over the radio, in daily conversations—that shrill barrage of slogans proclaiming that "there is only one Mexico."

Recently, when I expressed these views to an old friend, he smiled quite knowingly: "Let's face it, Hank, you're not really a Mexican—despite that long, comical name of yours. You're an American through and through." But that, of course, is a minority view and almost totally devoid of realism. One could just as well say that Martin Luther King is not a Negro, that he's merely an American. But the plain truth is that neither I nor Martin Luther King can escape the fact that we are a Mexican and a Negro whose roots are so deeply planted in the United States that we have grown those strong little hyphens that make us Mexican-American and Negro-American. This assertion may not please some idealists who would prefer to blind themselves to our obvious ethnic and racial differences, who are unwittingly patronizing when they insist that we are all alike and indistinguishable. But the politicians, undoubtedly the most pragmatic creatures in America, are completely aware that ethnic groups *do* exist and that they seem to huddle together, bitch together, and sometimes vote together.

When all is said and done, we hyphenated Americans are here to stay, bubbling happily or unhappily in the great nonmelting pot. Much has been gained and will be gained from the multiethnic aspects of the United States, and there is no useful purpose in attempting to wish it away or to homogenize it out of existence. In spite of the race riots in Watts and ethnic unrest elsewhere, there would appear to be a kind of modus vivendi developing on almost every level of American life.

And if there are those of us who may never feel completely at home, we can always make that brief visit to Bachimba.

Enrique Preciliano Lopez y Martinez de Sepulveda de Sapien, or Hank Lopez, a lawyer who now lives in New York, is co-editor of Dialogos, *a Mexican literary journal.*

Christmas at Chatsworth with Great-Granny Maud, Granny Evie, Mr. Erskine, Maud Baillie, the Duke and Duchess, fourteen children under the age of four, stables full of riding ponies, and a little piglet

By HAROLD MACMILLAN

In 1920 Harold Macmillan, then aide-de-camp to the Governor General of Canada, the ninth Duke of Devonshire, married the Duke's daughter, Lady Dorothy Cavendish. In his memoirs Britain's former prime minister recalls with particular warmth the celebration of Christmas at Chatsworth, his father-in-law's vast country house. This passage is quoted from the first volume of his memoirs, published by Harper & Row.

Perhaps in all the years the great period to which we most looked forward was Christmas. At first we spent these alternately with my parents at Birch Grove House or with my wife's family at Chatsworth. But as our children grew in number and age, and my parents saw how much my wife looked forward to the yearly reunion with her scattered family, my father and mother unselfishly pressed us to go to Chatsworth for Christmas, and to come to them at other times.

Christmas at Chatsworth was conducted on traditional lines. Every year was the same, except for the increasing number of children. The Devonshires' own family consisted, in addition to the Duke and Duchess, of two sons and five daughters, all married. A day or two before the festival, these began to arrive from different parts of the country.

The average number of children in each family was about four. These, with their attendant nursemaids, amounted therefore to something like fifty souls. Then there were the lady's maids and valets, bringing the total to at least sixty.

In addition there were other guests; sometimes my father and mother or other grandparents; sometimes "Great-Granny Maud," the Dowager Lady Lansdowne. There were others, too, who came year after year by long-established custom. There were generally two or three cousins of the Duke or Duchess. There was Mr. Erskine, Deputy Serjeant at Arms, the son of the great Serjeant at Arms who had been a lifelong friend of the Cavendishes; and Mr. Mansfield. These two had been Christmas guests from the times before the Duke succeeded, when he lived at Holker Hall in Lancashire. They were reputed intimate cronies of the Duke; he certainly treated them with more than his usual taciturnity. "Hello Jim," "Hello Walter," he would say when they arrived, and "Good-bye Jim" and "Good-bye Walter" when they left. So far as I know, no other conversation passed between them.

My much-loved sister-in-law, now Mary Dowager Duchess, came from a very different home and background. At first, I think, she found the long silences of the

CHATSWORTH
"No house is better fitted for roller skating."

Cavendishes somewhat trying; for she was a Cecil and Cecils talk all the time, about everything under the sun, with animated and fiercely contested verbal combats. The Duke did not like argument.

With all these Christmas visitors and their attendants, together with the permanent and temporary servants in the household, the number gathered under that vast roof must have been something like one hundred and fifty people. The children, of course, delighted in this strange and exciting world. They were spoiled and pampered by the servants and made long-lasting friendships with them. It was always a fresh pleasure to be conducted through the great kitchens, the huge pantries, the larders with their stone floors and vaulted roofs, and above all, the great building, larger than many butchers' shops, where hung rows of carcasses of oxen and sheep and game of every kind.

Many of the families, including my own, arrived with their ponies. So the stables were a continual source of interest, with each string of animals being accompanied by their attendant grooms.

The ritual did not differ from year to year. All assembled the day before. As each family arrived, "Granny Evie" received them at the top of the stairs where the Outer Hall led into the passageway to the great Painted Hall. My children still remember her greeting each family in turn—always in her place, as the cars passed the lodge—a gracious and dignified figure dressed in dark colors and long, flowing dresses, never changing. Shy and reserved as she was, with the children, like the Duke, she had no inhibitions.

The sons-in-law, of course, soon learned the desirability of sending their families by the early train and finding sufficient important business in London to make it necessary for them to follow later and more comfortably.

Christmas Day. Early to church at eight o'clock, crossing the park in the darkness; then breakfast and the morning with the enjoyment of minor presents. Balloons to be inflated, trumpets to be blown, and roller skates to be tried out. No house is better fitted for roller skating. The whole course is good, with particularly fast going on the stone floors of the Statue Gallery and the Orangery.

Then Matins at the parish church in the park, with a full and overflowing congregation, all the familiar hymns, and a mercifully short sermon. The clergyman likes to be asked to shoot, and the Duke, though he says little, has a good memory.

Christmas lunch, to which children above a certain age were allowed—the rules strictly enforced—and then the photograph. We all trooped out to a particularly cold and drafty part of the garden—by Flora's Temple, outside the Orangery. When at last all the generations could be brought into some kind of order, the yearly photograph was taken. Each year showed a steady increase and, happily, no casualties—not yet.

Boxing Day. The children who survived (there were always some who succumbed to colds or overexcitement) went off to the meet of the High Peak Harriers at Bakewell. At this time my sister-in-law Maud Baillie and her husband Evan were the Joint Masters. It was a great gathering of local sportsmen, coming from far and wide. There was no shooting on Boxing Day, so that all the men could enjoy their holiday. For those who did not hunt, it was a day of sleep, or bridge, or reading.

During the next few days there was shooting—and good shooting—and then some of the older members of the party began to disperse. But the mothers and children generally stayed on for two or three weeks, the fathers returning each weekend for more shooting. At last, reluctantly, but with a sense of great achievement, this large family party came to an end until the next year.

One year, as my wife reminds me, what she regards as the highest peak of felicity was reached—there were fourteen children under four years old in the nursery. Cavendishes have always liked children.

The old Duke, after his illness, became, except on rare occasions, gruff, unapproachable, even morose. But with children, especially little children, he was just the same as in old days. They were not afraid of him, and teased him, and took no notice of his disabilities. In return, he loved them dearly and spoiled them all. He even forgave them when they tripped over his gouty foot.

To go home to London or Sussex was almost as great an undertaking as to set out upon the Christmas journey. In addition to the quantities of luggage which everybody took about with them in those days, there were all the presents. One year, with rare unselfishness, I had agreed to travel back with my family. Besides everything else—children, nurses, servants, ponies, dogs, toys (mechanical and otherwise), and luggage—we brought back with us a little pig, which had been a gift to my eldest daughter. It was the runt of a litter on the home farm and had been given to her by her dear friend Mr. Shimwell, who managed almost everything at Chatsworth. It lived a long time in our nursery in Sussex, where it proved a clean, intelligent, and in every way desirable pet. It followed its mistress about everywhere with doglike devotion. It once fell into the swimming pool, and I acquired a high reputation among the children for courage, by jumping in and saving its life.

The Chatsworth gatherings lasted throughout all one decade and well into the next—indeed, until after the Duke's death in 1938. To remember them now is to recall another world, almost as remote from present-day England as the descriptions of Count Rostov's family in *War and Peace*.

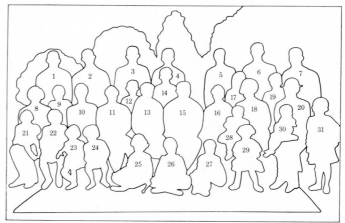

1. Lt. Col. Ivan Cobbold
2. The Rt. Hon. Harold Macmillan
3. Capt. Rt. Hon. James Stuart
   (now the Viscount Stuart of Findhorn)
4. Edward Cavendish, Marquess of Hartington
   and tenth Duke of Devonshire
5. Lady Anne Cavendish
6. Lord Charles Cavendish
7. Brig. the Hon. George Evan Baillie
8. Lady Blanche Cobbold
9. Pamela Maud Cobbold
10. Lady Dorothy Macmillan

11. Lady Rachel Stuart
    (now Viscountess Stuart of Findhorn)
12. Maurice Macmillan
13. The ninth Duchess of Devonshire
14. William Cavendish, Lord Hartington
15. The ninth Duke of Devonshire
16. The Dowager Marchioness of Lansdowne
17. Anne Mackintosh
18. The Marchioness of Hartington
    (now the Dowager Duchess of Devonshire)
19. Lord Andrew Robert Buxton Cavendish
    (the present Duke of Devonshire)
20. Lady Maud Baillie

21. John Cavendish Cobbold
22. Jean Cavendish Cobbold
23. Catherine Macmillan
24. The Hon. John Douglas Stuart
25. The Hon. David Randolph Stuart
26. Anne Caroline Macmillan
27. Lady Elizabeth Cavendish
28. Lady Anne Evelyn Cavendish
29. The Hon. Judith Baillie
30. The Hon. Peter Charles Baillie
31. The Hon. Michael Baillie
    (the present Baron of Burton)

In the shapes
and shadows
of an ancient city,
Franz Kafka
saw the terrors
of the
modern world

KAFKA'S PRAGUE

Shortly before Franz Kafka's death in 1924, a publisher in Prague planned to print two of his finest works, *The Trial* and *The Metamorphosis,* in a Czechoslovakian translation. Although the young author had lived in Prague nearly all his life, his publisher thought it necessary to add a preface to the volume, introducing Kafka to his own townspeople. Today, Kafka needs little preface, for his very name has been transformed into an adjective of world-wide currency: Kafkaesque. Without, perhaps, ever having read any of his works, modern man knows that Franz Kafka is the poet laureate of the horrors of the dehumanized, mechanized world, the world of alienation and isolation from all time and all place.

Kafka did not know all times and all places. He knew well, in fact, only one place, Prague—a city where even the shadows on a wall could be endowed with life (see opposite). His own life there began, one must suppose, on the same note that his book *The Trial* begins: "Someone must have slandered Josef K., because without his having done anything bad, he was arrested one fine morning."

Kafka's own trial began when he was born, as has often been pointed out, into a triple ghetto. He was a member of the Jewish minority, within the German minority, within the Czech minority of the Austro-Hungarian Empire. He lived principally in two quarters of Prague: the Old Town area, including the ghetto, and the realm of the immense Hradćany Castle—the symbol for him of vast, unapproachable, and incomprehensible authority—which contained a royal residence, the St. Vitus Cathedral, an administrative area staffed with government officials, and what amounted to a small town of private houses. It is the specter of Hradćany Hill that fills the settings of *The Trial* and *The Castle* and the spirit of the old ghetto that permeates the heroes thrust into those settings.

The trial of the fictional Josef K. never truly ends; it simply becomes, inexplicably, a sentence. At the close of the novel K. is escorted to his place of execution, stopping for a moment on a bridge where he looks lingeringly down on a small island. The bridge might well be the Charles Bridge; the island that of the Kampa, where Kafka sometimes sought peace. In the book, a knife is plunged into K.'s heart and, as though it were a ritual performed without passion, the knife is turned twice.

Kafka probably had no notion of becoming a prophet. Yet, his vision of Prague often seems to contain all the dark terrors that haunt today's world.

PICTORIAL ESSAY CONCEIVED AND PHOTOGRAPHED BY SONJA BULLATY AND ANGELO LOMEO

THE CASTLE

Although Kafka's original model for *The Castle* was probably a "rambling pile" of a castle he had known as a boy in his father's provincial home town of Wossek, his vision of it merged with Hradćany. And the High Court and government offices of *The Trial* clearly resided in Hradćany, where in reality, the inscrutable agents of an ancient monarchy kept themselves aloof from the rest of Prague. Opposite, at dusk, and overleaf, at night, the spires of St. Vitus Cathedral rise above the great castle. The Charles Bridge, below, and opposite seen reflecting the setting sun, joins Hradćany with the Old Town.

It was this theatrical setting that became, in Kafka's meticulous, lucid descriptions, so forbiddingly real. In *The Castle*, his hero, K., gazed up at the Castle and "could not help trying to put his own small experiences in relation to it . . ." For K. did not exist of himself; he existed only insofar as he had some relationship to the Castle. He was, as one might say of a modern bureaucrat, "defined by his function."

And what if that Castle or that function were to disappear? "When K. looked at the Castle, often it seemed to him as if he were observing someone who sat quietly there in front of him gazing, not lost in thought and so oblivious of everything, but free and untroubled . . . the gaze of the observer could not remain concentrated there, but slid away. This impression today was strengthened still further by the early dusk; the longer he looked, the less he could make out and the deeper everything was lost in the twilight."

THE OLD TOWN

Kafka grew up in Prague's Old Town—an area that could be as splendid as the Kinsky Palace, opposite, and as dilapidated as the courtyard overleaf. Both extremes are expressed in his novels. The children peering over the balustrade in the courtyard recall the youngsters in *The Trial* who looked at K. "angrily" when he disturbed their play on the steps. (He vowed to bring "sweets to cajole them with or else a stick to beat them" if ever he returned to the place.) One of the houses that Kafka himself lived in for a time is seen (overleaf, right) from the top of the tower of the Old Town Hall.

Kafka's father was a rugged, hard-driving businessman who ultimately owned a wholesale warehouse in the Kinsky Palace, an apartment block in the center of town, and a factory in the suburbs. His mother was a gentle woman, born of a family that had produced scholars and rabbis. The boy was fearful of his father, and, as he later wrote in his diary, unable to love his mother "as she deserved and as I might have . . ."

A stranger to his own family, Kafka wrote *The Metamorphosis*, the story of a child, Gregor Samsa, who awoke one morning from a dream and "found himself metamorphosed into a giant vermin." The story is confined to the reactions of Gregor's family to his hideous affliction. After months of trying to adjust to his condition (Kafka once noted in his diary, "I know how to accommodate myself to circumstances"), Gregor dies, and is swept out with the rubbish by the maid.

Kafka, considering himself as much an anomaly as Gregor, became, nonetheless, a lawyer, and rose, as his father would have wished, to more and more responsible positions with the insurance company that employed him. Still, his life often recalls the predicament of K. in *The Castle*, who had been engaged as a land surveyor and put to work as a janitor. And again, in *Amerika*, the young Karl, engaged as an actor, fears he will be put to work as a laborer. Franz Kafka had been "engaged" as a poet—and put to work as a minor bureaucrat.

In *The Trial*, a priest tells Josef K., who, like Kafka, is consumed by the law, this story: "Before the Law stands a doorkeeper. To this doorkeeper there comes a man from the country who begs for admittance to the Law. But the doorkeeper says that he cannot admit the man at the moment. The man, on reflection, asks if he will be allowed, then, to enter later. 'It is possible,' answers the doorkeeper, 'but not at this moment.' " The man peers through the door. The doorkeeper laughs: " 'If you are so strongly tempted, try to get in without my permission. But note that I am powerful. . . . From hall to hall, keepers stand at every door, one more powerful than the other.' " The man decides to wait. The doorkeeper gives him a stool, and he sits and waits—for years. Finally, old and dying, he thinks of a question he has never asked the doorkeeper: " 'Everyone strives to attain the Law . . . how does it come about, then, that in all these years no one has come seeking admittance but me?' The doorkeeper perceives that the man is nearing his end and his hearing is failing, so he bellows in his ear: 'No one but you could gain admittance through this door, since this door was intended for you. I am now going to shut it.' "

PRAGUE TODAY

Kafka's Prague lives on in modern Prague. Opposite, Saint Wenceslaus, in Wenceslaus Square, lifts his staff among the trolley wires. It was in this busy commercial center, now decorated by the Communist red star, that Kafka first worked. At the age of forty, Kafka died of tuberculosis and was buried in a cemetery belonging to the old synagogue whose serrated silhouette, above, rises over the former ghetto.

Kafka had come to detest his city—its commercial center, its ghetto, and Hradčany Hill. Yet he struggled always to imbue his nightmare vision of it with meaning and even hope. As his friend and biographer Max Brod wrote: "Through . . . Kafka's world, there sounds softly but unmistakably the note of love for the human creature who will 'nevertheless' not be abandoned—so runs the promise—by the divine powers . . ."

A Return to Manliness

*It's just like the days of old,
with long hair, and pinchy pants,
and all those other masculine things*

By J. H. PLUMB

To the middle-aged, long hair and effeminacy seem synonymous: the well-balanced, virile man was crew-cut in youth and close-cropped in age. Artists, weirdies, homosexuals, composed the long-haired brigade. Hence the sense of outrage in American and British homes when adolescent hair began to lengthen. Beatle mops might be cute on a five-year-old; at fourteen they were irritating; at eighteen an outrage. Yet worse is probably to come. Every Oxford and Cambridge college now has a dozen or so undergraduates with shoulder-length, Cavalier-style hair. Schools are steadily losing their fight to prescribe the clippers. After all, as the boys realize, no headmaster can send an entire school home. Even at Eton, hair is beginning to curl along the famous collar.

Since England is now the source of male fashion, the long-haired youth is going to disturb many more wholesome American households. Doubtless, like the female skirt, hair will have its ups and downs. But the betting must be on short skirts and long hair—both excite and infuriate for the same reason. If mothers and fathers knew their history, perhaps they would be less excited about the hair and more preoccupied with the deeper problems of the young male, particularly the affluent adolescent in a permissive society. Give young men money, and sooner or later they will dress like peacocks and behave like goats.

You can see them in the pictures of Pinturicchio: hair is shoulder-length;

tight, tight trousers emphasize muscular backsides; the stuffed codpiece with bright, laced points underlines an obvious virility; a short sword hangs from the waist; the taut alertness of their bodies adds foreboding. These youths played hide and seek with death, wantonly, arrogantly. They were the Oddi and Baglioni whose blood dyed the streets of Renaissance Perugia. They roamed through the streets, hacked each other to pieces, even killed each other in the Cathedral. And yet, they are as bright as parrots in their pinks and reds and greens, their hair dropping in scented ringlets to their shoulders; but for their high-styled codpieces they could easily be mistaken for girls, yet they were as ferociously virile as a herd of young bulls. And, of course, war was not—it never is—the only game they played. Affluent, leisured, these bourgeois-aristocrats hunted girls as well as rivals. Venice was littered with the brothels they frequented, and papal Rome did not lag far behind. And, of course, they experimented sexually.

But, you might argue, the Renaissance was a time of violent change, one of those exceptional epochs when an old morality was breaking down and when a new one had not yet emerged. No, Renaissance Italy was not the unique possessor of gaudy, aggressive, lascivious youngsters. In Elizabethan London young bloods maimed and murdered each other; pitched battles took place in Fleet Street and the Strand; Blackfriars Stairs, close by where Shakespeare lived, was a favorite spot for an ambush. The Montagues and Capulets of *Romeo and Juliet* were no strangers to Englishmen: they lived with them, and the Elizabethans saw, frequently enough, corpses of youths lying in their streets and alleys. Such feuds, like the violence of so much of the Elizabethan theatre, was natural to them. Sex, bloodshed, and horror were a part of the young male's life. And recall *these* Elizabethans—the scented lovelocks, the earrings (now coming back into fashion for English males), the pomanders hanging from the wrist,

the slashed and bejeweled doublets, the short cloak to show off the puffed-up breeches to advantage: there they strut like male birds of paradise.

Nor did the emergence of a stern puritanism keep them long in check. Charles II's courtiers were almost as wild and violent as their Elizabethan ancestors, and most of them just as young. The antics of young Rochester, standing stark-naked on a tavern balcony, were rip-roaring enough. The innocent were often victims—beaten, hunted, sometimes killed, all for a night's sport. And this was the way, too, of the Mohocks, mere boys, who terrorized Londoners in Queen Anne's day, uncontrollable youths for whom law and order was an anathema. And their dress was as exhibitionistic as their behavior. Indeed, it remained so until good Queen Victoria's days. The Macaronis and Corinthians, the young, riotous friends of the Prince of Wales, were just as obstreperous, just as wildly exhibitionistic, at the end of the eighteenth century as the Mohocks were at the beginning of it. Perhaps youth was even more violent then than it is today. Few schools now riot and need the militia to quell them—as did Eton, Winchester, and Harrow.

And it is the same story with sex as with violence—precocity all the way. That Juliet was fifteen astonished no one in Shakespeare's audience: for them, pubescent girls were fair game. In the eighteenth century William Hickey—a cherubic, lovely boy with a soft, peachlike complexion and long, girlish, curly hair—was familiar, at fourteen, with all the Covent Garden brothels. Add to this his penchant for the bottle and his uncontrollable lust for gambling, and we have a picture of a not untypical rich, bourgeois boy of the eighteenth century. His friends, and he was very popular, only differed from Hickey in the extent of their excesses. Nor was this a vice of Anglo-Saxon youth. It is an aspect of at least the last five centuries of the European scene. Britain's youths had their parallels from Italy to Sweden.

And they are still with us, or rather they are back with us after a temporary absence of a generation or so. Any evening in England, one will see figures cased in black, hair shoulder-length: nail-studded belts, tight, tight black jeans, leather coats padded to emphasize the shoulders, scarlet crash helmets swinging from the wrist. And straight down the right buttock a long sheath knife, not meant as an ornament. By their side, huge motorbikes that snarl and leap and roar. Rockers out for Mods: the Oddi out for the Baglioni, the Capulets after the Montagues, the Mohocks riding again. And down in Carnaby Street the boys of sixteen are buying flowered shirts, sniffing new scents, wondering if eye shadow is in or not. Beastly decadence? No, the everlasting problem of the sexually mature adolescent one finds in all societies affluent enough to fill the pockets of the young male.

This is not a problem of our society; it is a problem of humanity, made worse, it may appear, because we are richer and more numerous today. True, we intensify it somewhat by publicity and by our lack of any sense of proportion. Percentagewise, our own long-haired youths are far less violent, murderous, and intolerable than their historic counterparts. The situation, however, goes deeper than our social structure. And we shall not solve it by exhortation or repression. The problem, if it is a problem, might be eased if parents, headmasters, and the like took changes in young male exhibitionism more lightheartedly. It might help, too, if aging men grew less choleric when faced by the all-too-obvious evidence of youthful virility. But the problem will still be there, so long as we are affluent and free from a rigidly imposed state morality. Without that there will be student battles on the beaches, drunkenness, sex orgies. Since before Samson's day, long hair and virility have been, shall we say, bedfellows.

Professor J. H. Plumb's chair of history at Christ College, Cambridge, provides an excellent vantage point from which to observe the ever-changing appearance of Young England.

James Stuart (1612–1655) and John Emelin (1945–   ) consider their cultural ties.

THE GYPSY'S TREASURE

A bracelet on a pretty Spanish arm led archaeologists to an ancient trove of gold

A gold bracelet on the arm of a pretty gypsy in a town in southeastern Spain has led to the discovery of a three-thousand-year-old treasure which may alter the entire concept of prehistoric civilization in western Europe.

The treasure consists of bracelets, bowls, and flagons, all of intricately worked pure gold; and one flagon of iron with gold overlay (the earliest iron piece ever to be found in the peninsula) is unique in Europe. Nothing to compare with it has ever been found before. Most significant, the workmanship is distinctly western European, without any parallel whatsoever to the goldsmith's art of the early Aegean civilizations with which it was contemporary.

It was on an October day in 1963 that a jeweler in the Spanish town of Villena was chatting with a young gypsy woman and observed that she wore an extraordinarily beautiful bracelet. Could he have a look at her bracelet? the jeweler asked; and upon examining the heavy, elaborately incised armpiece more closely, he saw it was of pure gold. He immediately summoned the director of Villena's museum of archaeology, Señor José Maria Soler. Señor Soler, becoming even more excited than the jeweler, asked the gypsy where her bracelet came from. She replied that her husband had found it in some sand that was being used to mix concrete.

A month later another gypsy woman was seen wearing a heavy gold bracelet. Hers was a family treasure, she insisted, which her grandmother had found wedged between the stones of their old house. But when Señor Soler examined her "heirloom," he saw that, like the other bracelet, it bore fresh traces of soil. Believing the gypsies had accidentally uncovered a prehistoric find, the archae-

ologist obtained legal permission to confiscate both bracelets until their origin could be determined. Soon after, the husband of the second gypsy, a construction worker named Juan Calatayud, confessed that he himself had found both bracelets while working in a gravel quarry. He volunteered to lead the archaeologist to the spot, a *rambla*, or ravine, near Villena.

Señor Soler knew the region well, for while excavating nearby, he had already found evidence of an extensive Bronze Age industry which had produced textiles as well as metal goods in the latter part of the second millennium B.C. Only six months earlier what is now called a "little treasure" of gold objects had been unearthed by workers in a gypsum quarry on a hill known as Cabezo Redondo. Scattered deep in the chalky soil along with pottery sherds and other shattered prehistoric remains, this find consisted of gold rings, three bracelets (smaller than but stylistically similar to those worn by the two gypsy women), many small gold studs which might once have held precious stones for a crown or scepter, a flexible diadem of gold, and, most interesting of all, a number of unfinished pieces and a bar of unworked gold bearing the outline of a pattern. Surely a goldsmith's shop or factory had once stood here.

The bracelets Juan Calatayud had found were so like the Cabezo Redondo pieces that they must certainly have been made by the same highly skilled goldsmith. Señor

Among the most beautiful of the Villena treasures are a gold flagon (opposite, top), several unfinished rings, looking very much like modern wedding bands, three finely decorated bowls, an ornament with gold inlays, and four heavy bracelets. The largest is the one the gypsy woman was wearing.

By BETTY WASON

Soler rounded up four men who had helped him at Cabezo Redondo, and on the first of December, a windy, sharp day, they started clearing an area a hundred feet square in the *rambla*, meticulously digging down through gravelly loam to heavy red clay soil and working their way into the hillside from the spot indicated by the gypsy. By sunset they had found nothing, and were about to give up for the day when one of the men cried out. He had found another heavy gold bracelet! Moments later they came upon a huge pottery jar which, once the soil had been cleared away, proved to be filled to the brim. Even in the swiftly fading light, the glint of gold was dazzling.

They dared not leave the spot. After building a bonfire for warmth, they sent one of the men back to Villena for a photographer and more equipment. The vessel was so large and so deeply buried that it was nine o'clock that night before they could extricate it.

Back in Villena they found that the jar contained sixty-six separate pieces: twenty-eight bracelets, eleven bowls, five flagons—two of gold, two of silver, the fifth of iron (as precious as gold in the prehistoric era). In addition there were buttons or ornaments of lead worked with gold, one decorated with amber, and several unidentified objects, some of which appeared to be sword handles. The total weight of the gold treasure was twenty-two pounds—the heaviest ever unearthed. One bracelet alone weighed 465 grams, more than a pound.

The jar had been so skillfully packed that not an inch of space was wasted. This fact, and the great depth at which the jar was buried, suggest that it was a king's treasure which had been buried for safekeeping. Evidence of fire in the soil around the spot indicated that a building once stood there, perhaps a royal palace which was set ablaze in the course of a battle.

As carefully as the jar was packed, it had no lid, and over the centuries the currents of underground rivulets had dislodged some of the bracelets on top and carried them deeper into the ravine. It was these bracelets that Juan Calatayud had found.

What king owned this precious treasure? Señor Soler theorizes that he was one of many petty rulers in southern Spain during the late Bronze Age and that, like other kings, he had his own private army and his own master goldsmith who supervised other metalworkers. He must have lived in the same sort of splendor as the Mycenaean princes, or King Alcinous, who, according to Homer, ate from dishes of silver and gold. The golden bowls and flagons were probably royal tableware.

Perhaps soldiers hired to defend the kingdom were recompensed for valor with treasures of gold—a practice which would explain why three other articles, enough alike to have been made by the Villena goldsmith, have turned up in widely scattered places: two strikingly similar bracelets have been found in Portugal, and near Zurich a golden bowl which matches one of the Villena bowls in color and shape. Whether or not these pieces were actually made in Villena, they reflect the same style or fashion and unquestionably belong to the same period.

Many Greek and Roman writers described Spain as having the richest gold, silver, and copper mines in the ancient world. Hundreds of bronze pieces dating from 1500 B.C. have been found in the peninsula. Three other significant gold treasures have also been found—but all from the sixth century B.C. (much later than the Villena hoard) and all identified as jewels of Tartessus.

The kingdom of Tartessus reached its peak from the eighth to the sixth century B.C., but it was completely destroyed by invading Phoenicians and Carthaginians in the sixth century B.C., and to this day the site of its capital city has not been located. The discovery of the three Tartessian gold treasures as well as princely Tartessian graves indicates that the capital lay in the region of Cadiz or Seville. When the Villena discoveries were first announced, some archaeologists thought that they might belong to an early period of Tartessus, despite the fact that Tartessus was almost surely in the southwest, while the new find cropped up in the southeast. But the jewels of Tartessus were of ornate design, bearing such typically Oriental figures as palmettes, hawks, lions, and lotus flowers. The Villena gold treasures are exquisitely simple, marked only with geometric patterns. Further, they pre-date the Tartessus jewels by at least three or four hundred years, having been produced around 1,000 B.C. and certainly no later than the early ninth century—a date arrived at by comparing the newly found treasure with the pottery and bronze artifacts found at Cabezo Redondo.

Some see a likeness to later Celtic jewelry in the Villena treasure, and since the first wave of Celts reached southern Spain in the ninth century B.C., there has been some speculation that this might be the earliest representation of Celtic art. But the Celts would have found an already established Bronze Age civilization here, and it is more likely that the roots of this culture go much farther back, perhaps even to the unknown artists who sketched pictures of cattle herders, archers, and dancing women on rock ledges in eastern Spain some eight thousand years ago. The search for more clues has of course been intensified. It is possible that future finds will uncover a uniquely Western civilization which developed in the Iberian Peninsula and remained totally independent of the Mycenaean and Egyptian cultures.

Betty Wason, an editor and Hispanophile, is the author of a culinary history, Cooks, Gluttons, and Gourmets.

History in the Telephone Book

The Manhattan Directory has its strongest roots in the Norman Conquest

By C. M. MATTHEWS

Few people look at a telephone directory for any other reason than to find a number or an address, but a student of surnames can read it for pleasure, discovering human history in its close-packed columns. Anyone turning the pages of the Manhattan directory can see a population composed of many races. The salient points are obvious, but some specialized knowledge is required to interpret the details.

In the 1963–64 edition of this solid book, which contains about 800,000 entries, the first twenty-five surnames are, in numerical order: Smith, Brown, Johnson, Williams, Cohen, Miller, Jones, Schwartz, Davis, Green, White, Harris, Lee, Levine, Levy, Wilson, Lewis, Rodriguez, Friedman, Taylor, Clark, Robinson, Klein, Jackson, Martin, slight variations of spelling that do not affect the sound being ignored. The entry counts of these outstanding names vary from 3,160 to just under a thousand. Six of them are Jewish or German in origin, one Spanish, and the remaining eighteen, or 72 per cent, are British, or to be more precise, English and Welsh. No purely Scottish name qualifies for this short list, but numerous Scots are included among the Wilsons and Johnsons, typical North of England names which are shared with the Lowlands of Scotland. Some of these British names are now borne by families of non-British origin, including Negro families, but they stem nonetheless from the English past.

It may surprise some that no Irish name is included, but the Irish, who developed fixed surnames even earlier than the English, have wonderful variety in their highly distinctive names, so that their numbers are dissipated among many forms. In this directory, for instance, there are more than six hundred different surnames beginning with Mac- or Mc-, the majority of them Irish, though some of course are Scots. The commonest Irish surname, which is Murphy, scores under eight hundred.

In direct contrast to the Irish, the Welsh,

who were much later in acquiring permanent surnames, have most of their numbers concentrated in a few favorites, with the result that they have become extremely prominent throughout the English-speaking world. Of those on our list, Lewis, though sometimes derived from the French Louis, is generally Welsh in origin. It signifies "the son of Llewi," a shortened form of Llewellyn, a name beloved by all Welshmen as that of their last sovereign independent prince. Davis, too, owes most of its numbers to Welsh loyalty, this time to the patron saint of Wales; but David was a popular Christian name in medieval England also, and many surnames were formed from it both there and in Scotland at that time. Jones is simply the Welsh pronunciation of the English Johns. Williams was an English surname in the Middle Ages but was later augmented by countless Welsh families, who have overflowed into England ever since the accession of the half-Welsh Tudors to the throne in the latter part of the fifteenth century.

The large Jewish element in the population of Manhattan is clearly indicated by the high position on our list of Cohen and Levy (with its variant form, Levine), Hebrew names designating offices of the priesthood. But the Jews have often been inclined to use the surnames of the country they live in, particularly the names that involve only a slight alteration of a name of their own; in this way many of them have

Page Georgia 315W113 .... MO 6-9750
Page Gilbert E 201E25 689-7828
Page Girl Togs Inc 101W31 .... PE 6-0930
Page Glenn R 620E20 .... ALgnqn 4-0717
Page Gloria ... 2160MadAv .... AU 1-0160
Page G... 595MadAv 421-8190
Page H... SqVilg 982-9717
Page Ha... thur atty 391E14 .... CY 2-2244
Page ... 605W184 923-4349
Page ... 501W141 ...brn 4-3271
Page H... ...W14... .... SA 3...34
Page H... W14... Win...
Page H... .... OR 5-4754
Page H...
1160 ... tPlnsRd Mamk ...143
Page ... 528W152 .... AUg... ...221
Page ... 121E31 .... WUryhil 6-7318
Page ... 0E106 .... TR 6-6518
Page ... 151E80 .... RE 4-2456
Page ... ev 1W127 .... FI 8-0924
Page ... 1AmstrdmAv 926-8723
Page ... 1W137 .... Drndak 4-3552
Page J... 9E57 755-7159
Page ...R ...E38 697-3899
Page ...as Ray ...5Rutgrs 267-2417
Page Jas W ...3W131 281-3403
Page Jane N M 149E38 .... Uryhil 5-6359
Page Jessie 25 W137 281-1185
Page John 137... .... UN 1-7264
Page John 101W12 691-6342
Page John 126E28 3-6147
Page John D 191AudbnAv .... SW 5-8256
Page John N Jr 142E33 684-1816
Page L C&Co 19UnionSq .... OR 5-3000

Harp R Wm 325WstEndAv........... EN 2-3981
Harp Raleigh 114W70 .... TR 4-0296
Harp Rush 288W12 .... CH 2-8376
Harp Salon 109W57 .... CI 7-6285
Harp Thos 309E99 ....TRaflgr 6-6407
Harpas Alexndr Rev 70LaSal 662-3045
Harpel Jas W 201E66 988-7920
Harpel Peter MD 4... .... YU 2-454/
Harper A hrdwr ...W2 .....WAtkns 9-7453
Harper A Mrs 120W1... .....MOnumnt 2-6536
Harper A R 820W1... .... RE 7-3491
Harper Aaron J 317... .....ADrndak 4-1480
Harper Affiliates .... YU 6-2515
Harper Agnes C ... ...GH...elsea 3-3519
Harper Albert 1... 3-1509
Harper Albert L... 2-5065
Harper Alfonso... ...64-5060
Harper Alfred,... .....E 4-8160
Harper Aliso... .....A 9-6836
Harper Andr... Ra...lgr 3-9159
Harper And... ...3 ..... MU 6-1627
Harper An... 744-7061
Harper A... .... WA 6-9199
Harper A... 795-3503
Harper Ar... ...lOnumnt 2-1476
Harper Ass... 689-9090
Harper-Atlan... .....5Av .... YU 6-3344
Harper Aubrey .... TR 6-7693
Harper&Bateman r...
... 84J...us Bklyn DI 2-5565
Harper Beatrice Mr... 479W14... ... AU 3-3805
Harper Bertram 5...W147 862-3010
Harper Billie J 813StNchlasAv ...., AU 6-0842
Harper Billy W 96 5Av .... CH 3-6537
Harper&Brothers pubrs 49E33 889-7500

Knight Dinah L
  CordwdPath SaintJames .... 516 JU 4-5723
Knight ... 238E50 .... HA 1-3286
Knig... ... REctr 2-1314
Knight ...ld B Mrs 200E66 ...TEmpir 8-5819
Knig... ... AU 1-4413
Knight ...ra 26...Av 873-6831
Knight D... J...34W122 ...UNivrsty 5-0081
Knight Dor... 5Av 777-4014
Knight E A ... . CH 3-9195
Knight E A 243-5255
Knight Ear... .... LEhi 4-4308
Knight&Ec... ...20Bway .... RE 2-1314
Knight E 243-7351
Knight E 255-0463
Knight E ...92 .... UN 5-0631
Knight ...4W1... .... AU 6-2892
Knight ... . UN 5-1715
Knight ... . TR 7-5030
Knigh... ...W1... .... AU 6-6762
Knigh... 475-8188
Knig... ...enc... 41..W144 .....dak 4-5114
Knight ... 5A... ....za 8-1441
Knight F... 25...trlPk... .... CI 5-4386
Knight Fe...e Co...c 36...Kngsbr... ...XI 8-4400
Knight Flo...nce ...870C...mbusAv ...nt 6-8111
Knight Fl...ce ... 2640 8...v .....bn 6-9238
Knight Fr...k H ...577 712
Knight...ank L Rev ...StNchla... 09
Knight Fred 500W1... 92
Knight G A 66E119 043
Knight Gail 55E99 722-9684
Knight Gary b 48StNichAv .... RI 9-7953
Knight Geo 564LenoxAv .... ADrndak 4-4383

adopted Lewis, Davis, and other British surnames, greatly increasing their numbers in New York. Many of the most distinctive Jewish surnames are German, and spring from edicts of the late eighteenth and early nineteenth century in several Germanic states, particularly Austria, where Jews were compelled to take permanent surnames of a sort not readily confused with traditionally Teutonic names. Jewish families naturally chose pleasant themes, though some of them had to make sizable payments to be registered under the names of their choice. The results may be seen in the many columns of Friedman (man of peace), Rosenbaum, (rose tree), Greenberg (green mountain), Goldstein (gold stone), and so forth. These surnames, deliberately chosen in comparatively modern times, differ in their origin from those that had developed much earlier in Germany as a natural growth (many of them nicknames, such as "Klein" meaning "little"), and earlier still in England, France, and Italy.

We may look in vain for large blocks of Italian names. Like those of the Irish, they are diversified in endless slightly varied forms, and though there are plenty of them scattered through the directory, hardly any reach a hundred examples. For instance, "Rossi," a common nickname for a red-headed man, may also have taken the form of Rosso, Rossini, Rossetti, Rosselli, or other variations arising from colloquial use. It may also have been abbreviated to Ross, which in English usage implied an origin from one of several places so named in the Celtic West. Spanish surnames, on the other hand, include large numbers of patronymics in regular, unvaried form, of which Rodriguez ("son of Rodrigo") is the most common.

If we were to continue with our statistics and classify all the surnames in the directory according to their racial origins, we would find all the nations of the world represented in due proportion, telling the story of immigration into the great city of New York during the past three centuries. But if we concentrate on the British element, we will find something of the history of England from a much earlier date. For English surnames reflect the social backgrounds of the people who bore them centuries before the *Mayflower* sailed.

Many do not realize the antiquity of the great mass of English surnames. Those that have received the most attention are the aristocratic Norman names, like Beauchamp, Devereux, and Neville, that can frequently be traced back to the time of the Conquest and before, and genealogists have sometimes led us to believe that the English were far behind the Normans in their use of surnames. A study of some of the medieval documents that include the names of large numbers of ordinary people will prove otherwise. Thousands of undertenants, both English and Norman, are named in Domesday Book; a few eleventh- and twelfth-century manorial rolls give the names of mere peasants; assizes of arms, beginning in 1181, deal with all freemen; and the series of subsidy rolls, recording nationwide taxation instigated by Edward I after his accession in 1272, give copious and detailed evidence of the state of surnames in his reign.

Anyone who studies these sources will discover that the system of fixed surnames for all the population evolved slowly but early; that both for rich and poor, whether English or Norman, it began about the time of the Conquest; that by 1200 almost everyone was equipped with a second name, though many still changed them; that by 1300 the majority of names were permanent; and that the following century saw the process virtually complete for all. Since that time some families have changed their names, but they are a tiny minority compared with those who have not done so. In short, the majority of English surnames date from the period between the Battle of Hastings and the birth of Chaucer.

Returning to the eighteen British names that score the highest on our list, we find that they are typical of their country of origin and can be found in large numbers in every English city. Every one of these eighteen is included in the top thirty of the London Telephone Directory, and fifteen of them are in the top twenty, appearing almost in the same order as in the

Weller Drug Store 325MadAv .... MU 7-1790
Weller E E Co 47W34 .... LA 4-1446
Weller Elec Corp expt 13E40 .... MU 9-0200
Weller Eli S 258RivDr .... MO 3-7896
Weller F B DDS ofc 515MadAv .ELdorado 5-5885
Weller Fabrics Inc 54W57 .... CI 7-3790
Weller Francis J b 420LexAv .... MU 3-7417
Weller Harry 440WEndAv .... EN dicot 2-0920
Weller Henry J Co acctnts 405ParkAv.. EL 5-0390
Weller Howard W 115BenettAv ..... LOraln 8-5766
Weller J 1370StNchlasAv 781-8377
Weller J A c'n Co brkrs 90WBway ..... WO 2-2910
Weller J I 3 .0E50 .... MUryhil 8-0090
Weller J   .0E62 838-18
Weller   0ParkAv 427-2755
..IN RESEARCH INC
..felrPlz. JU 2-044
.... CI 7-
.... AT 9-7287
.... AC 2-3782
...... REgnt 4-6673
..... GRmrcy 3-1259
..... REgnt 7-2202
.... MU 7-1790
..ller Ralph H 225E56 .... MU 3-8319
..ller Robt A Corp 261 5 .... OR 9-1162
..eller Robt B brkr 25 road ...... WH 3-7700
..Res 1070ParkAv .... FI 8-0705
..eller Sida 123E7 .... UN 1-7094
..eller Sigmund 50 Bway ...rain
Weller Theo 405E56 753-5316
Weller V I 150WstEndAv 362-9110
Weller V I 305W72 .... TR-7-2615
Weller Wm H Inc 149Bway .... WO 2-2235

Manhattan directory. What is more, they are also to be found in the first English parish registers, which date from 1538, and can be seen in earlier forms in the medieval documents already mentioned.

The only marked difference in the numerical order of surnames from the Tudor period to the present day is the increase of the Welsh representation. In the registers of the reign of Elizabeth I, Jones, Williams, and Davis can be found only in small numbers and Lewis hardly at all, except in western counties bordering Wales, where all are plentiful. At this time English surnames were already old-established and, having originated as fragments of daily speech, echoed the colloquialisms of earlier days. Therefore patronymics formed from popular names came frequently from familiar forms and abbreviations. William far more often produced Wills, Wilson, Wilkins, Wilkes, and other variations than the straightforward Williams; David gave the surnames Davey, Davison, Dawson, and Dawkins, as well as Davis. Robert was generally turned into Robin, resulting not only in Robbins and Robinson but also in rhymed forms like Dobbs and Hobbs. Richard became not only Dick but Hick, giving us surnames like Dickens and Hickson and many more. In England, as in Italy and France, every popular Christian name split into a profusion of well-diversified forms. But the Welsh, like several other peoples who adopted hereditary patro-

nymics at a later date, formed them as possessives of the full Christian name—Jones and Hughes, Evans and Edwards, are common results.

The great popularity in England of the names William, Robert, and Henry was due to the Conqueror and his sons, and although these names were alien and probably hateful to the English at first, such was the prestige of royalty and feudal power that by 1200 they were the commonest names in England. Even the name of a bad king was sure to filter down to all classes eventually, and if it also belonged to an important saint, who might offer some protection to the bearer, so much the better. By 1300 John had surpassed William in favor, and it is only natural that derivatives of John, including Jackson, should make up three entries on our list, with two derivatives of William appearing. Robert was next in order in the thirteenth century, its vogue, started by the Normans, being aided in later centuries by the exploits of the English folk hero Robin Hood. It comes a little lower than Henry on our list because it branched into so many forms, among which its numbers are divided; whereas Henry, which was universally pronounced Harry, occurs nearly always in the form of Harris or Harrison.

The one remaining patronymic on our list, Martin, was one of the few Continental names used in England before the Con-

quest. The Anglo-Saxons were conservative in the use of their own ancient name-system, in which the frequent repetition of the same elements, such as Aethel-, Aelf-, and Ead-, is extremely confusing to modern readers. They held the great figures of the Bible in too much reverence to use their names, except occasionally for priests, and the first saints' names that they gave to their children belonged to holy men who had lived comparatively near them in time and space. Saint Martin was an early favorite. By legend a Roman soldier who divided his cloak with a beggar and learned in a vision that he had shared it with Christ, he was actually a French bishop who played an important part in the conversion of Gaul in the fourth century. His shrine at Tours became a place of pilgrimage, and the monastery he founded there had many early links with England. It happened also that his special day, Martinmas, fell on November 11, close to the ancient festival of the dying year, and thus his cult became associated with feasting and conviviality. One way or another, the name of Martin was well loved in Anglo-Saxon England, and when at last the old native names began to give way to foreign influences, it came quickly into general use, reaching the height of its popularity in the century after the Conquest.

Devotion to Saint Martin was widespread in western Europe. The French have exactly the same surname, varied with Martineau

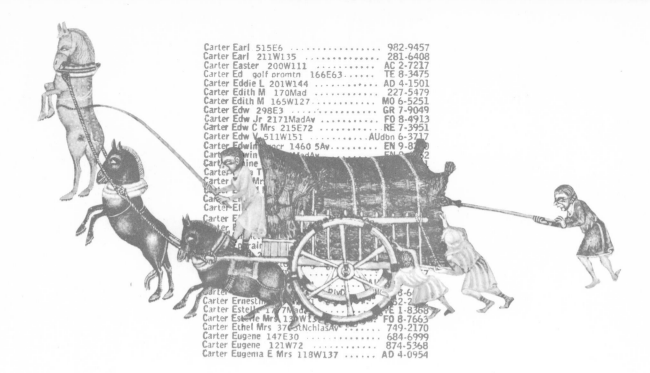

Carter Earl 515E6 982-9457
Carter Earl 211W135 281-6408
Carter Easter 200W111 .... AC 2-7217
Carter Ed golf promtn 166E63...... TE 8-3475
Carter Eddie L 201W144 .... AD 4-1501
Carter Edith M 170Mad 227-5479
Carter Edith M 165W127 .... MO 6-5251
Carter Edw 298E3 .... GR 7-9049
Carter Edw Jr 2171MadAv .... FO 8-4913
Carter Edw C Mrs 215E72 .... RE 7-3951
Carter Edw V 511W151 .... AUdbn 6-3717
Carter Edwin ocr 1460 5Av .... EN 9-8___
Carter Edwin ____ MadAv ....EN _ ___ _2
Cart_ _ ine
Carter __ a T
Carter __ Mr_
Ca___ En
Carter El_
Carter E___
_er E___

Carter Ernest ____ ___ __ 8-6___
Carter Estell_ 17_7Mad ___ __ ___ 32-2___
Carter Este_le Mrs 13_W15_ ___ RE 1-8368
Carter Esterle Mrs 13_W15_ ____ FO 8-7663
Carter Ethel Mrs 37 StNchlasAV 749-2170
Carter Eugene 147E30 684-6999
Carter Eugene 121W72 874-5368
Carter Eugenia E Mrs 118W137 ...... AD 4-0954

and other forms. The Italians have Martini, Martinetti, and many more, while among New Yorkers of Spanish stock, Martinez is second in numerical order.

In England Martin, which is the fourteenth most common surname in London, has produced hardly any variations, seldom even carrying the final "s" or "son" so common with patronymics. The reason for this is that Martin was established as a surname too early for such additions. All the oldest patronymics are without suffixes, surnames like Edgar, Elgar, Oswald, Alwyn, Thurston, and many more that were Christian names before the Conquest. It is true that in that period men were often called by their fathers' names with the addition of "son," and that this was occasionally written as one word, but far more often it was expressed as an ordinary statement of fact in two separate words, and plentiful evidence shows that when it passed on to another generation for which it was no longer true, the "son" and possessive "s" dropped off, leaving the original Christian name to continue as a permanent surname without any appendage whatever. Thus "Godwines sune," as it was written in the eleventh century, survives only as Godwin or Goodwin. The only pre-Conquest names that did undergo some changes were Edward and Edmund, which were deliberately revived by Henry III for his sons, thus bringing them into line with the Norman favorites, and Cuthbert, which survived just long enough in the north, where the seventh-century saint's life was remembered, to form a few Cuthbertsons. It was not until the thirteenth century, when the great mass of the working people were acquiring fixed surnames and every possible variety of form was needed to differentiate one man from another, that these final tags reappeared and adhered in large numbers, "son" being more common in the north and "s" in the south and west. But before this happened, Martin and several others of the same vintage, such as Austin (the English version of Augustine), had dropped out of fashion as first names.

It was a strange phenomenon that had caused the personal names of the Anglo-Saxons to disappear so completely, something deeper than mere fashion. Two centuries after the Conquest, they had gone, most of them forever, and though a few were revived in the nineteenth century, the vast majority are unknown today. And yet these forgotten names are still with us, scattered through the pages of the telephone directory as living links with a remote past. They are not easy to recognize without some knowledge of Anglo-Saxon, and they are much eroded by time, but they are more plentiful than one might expect. A few examples are as follows: Alston comes from Athelstan, Alden from Ealdwine, Aylward from Aethelward, Sewell from Sigweald, Wolsey from Wulfsig, Kimball and Kemble from Cynebeald, Goodrich from Godric, and Etheridge from Aethelric. Such names are the oldest of all our patronymics and commemorate English families who clung sturdily to their own traditions when Norman influence was becoming paramount.

From patronymics we turn now to the four surnames, high on our list, that are taken from occupations. Smith, Miller, Taylor, and Clark are also the first four in this classification in London, Toronto, Sydney, and probably every large English-speaking community, their high numbers accurately reflecting the most essential services of the medieval world.

It is with good reason that Smith is the foremost English name. The conditions that caused a particular occupation to make a common surname were, first, that it had to supply a vital need, so that it would be found in every part of the country, and, second, that it was rare enough within each group to be outstanding. The smith fulfilled both these conditions. The lives of the whole community depended on his skill for the weapons of hunting and war and for the tools of agriculture. He is the medieval representative of applied science; and the baron in his castle, wanting repairs for his armor, was as interested in the smith as the peasant needing a new spade.

The miller, who ground the grain for bread, was another essential figure. One might expect as many millers as smiths, for there was a miller in every village of any size, but he could only function in his mill, whereas a smith would be found in every castle, every baron's retinue, every soldiers' camp. In New York Miller is higher (sixth) than it is in London (nineteenth), owing to the fact that some German Müllers have anglicized the spelling of their names. The meaning of the two forms is of course identical, the only difference being that the ancestor from whom the name derives kept his mill either by an English stream in the thirteenth century or earlier, or by a German one a good deal later. If your name is Milner it was fixed at the earliest date of all, for "mylnere" is the Anglo-Saxon form of the word, which was gradually contracted to "miller" after the Conquest.

It must be noted that it was special skill and equipment which gave these men their importance. Compared with them, mere tillers of the soil were totally undistinguished. Every man in a village had his strips in the common field and could guide the heavy plow, so there was little point in calling a man a plowman, though it was bound to happen occasionally. In the Manhattan directory there is just one Plowman, but there are more than three thousand of the men who forged the plowshare and more than two thousand of those who ground the grain.

We come now to the tailor, who has a surprising numerical importance (the Taylors on our list run to four figures). Surely, it may be said, in a primitive community many essentials would come before fine clothes. But this assumes that the word meant then what we mean by it today. The tailor of the twelfth and thirteenth centuries made all the clothing a man required, including coverings, generally of soft leather, for the feet and legs. The word was a Norman importation meaning literally "cutter," which replaced the Old English "shearer" and "suter" who had cut and stitched in even earlier times. As the new word became established, so shearer was narrowed in meaning to the cutting of sheep's wool, while "soutar" (or "sutter") lingered on in the north, applying to an old-fashioned shoemaker. Meanwhile, the loose tunics that had been made largely by the womenfolk in the Saxon and early Norman periods gave way to better-fitting garments, increasing the work of the tailor so that the making of footwear, which had once been his principal task, split off as a separate craft. The first specialists in this business were the cordwainers, who made luxury shoes of imported cordovan for the rich. But luxury trades, found only in large towns, never produced many surnames; it is the small village community, multiplied by thousands, that has filled our directories. The fashionable cordwainers have provided just four Cordners in Manhattan and six in London. Shoemaking for the masses did not become a separate craft until the fifteenth century, which was too late to make surnames in England, and there are none

at all in London; but in Germany, as we have seen, surnames became fixed later, so that both Schumacher and Schumann are well known there and in America.

No one need think that these early craftsmen—the smith, the miller, the tailor, and others of the same type, such as the builder (Wright), the weaver (Webster), and the cooper, who made barrels and tubs—were of very low degree. In an age when most of the population were peasants tilling the soil and tied to it in semibondage, these craftsmen ranked as freemen. Their abilities had already raised them above their fellow villagers; they had opportunities to prosper, and many of them did so at an early date.

The clerk had a totally different kind of skill. Trained in the monastery, he could read and write—rare accomplishments, in Norman England, that placed him in the professional class. Many early Clarks must have earned their names with but a modicum of learning; others were the influential secretaries on whom kings, barons, and bishops relied for the management of their affairs. It must be remembered that at this time the higher orders of the clergy were supposed to be celibate. It cannot truthfully be said that they always were so, but at least the founding of families among them was kept to moderate proportions, and the enormous influence of the Church on medieval life is reflected only obliquely in our surnames. Exalted names of high

Smith Roger D 30 5Av	GRmrcy 5-3653
Smith Roger D lwvr 2Wall	REctr 2-3200
Smith Roger E 500E77	NA 8-4143
Smith Roger H 92Grove	OR 5-1836
Smith Roger Hotel LexAv&47	PL 5-1400
Smith Roger P 220E54	EL 5-1454
Smith Roger W 231W25	243-1213
Smith Roland Jr 310E71	249-5506
Smith Rola... 217?MadAv	AUdbn 1-2847
Smith... W110	UN 6-3146
Smith Ro?e...	MO 1-3694
Smith Roth	OR 4-8964
Smith Rome...	MOnumnt 6-3170
Smith Romo...	WAdswth 6-5821
...mith Ron...	WO 2-8000
...th Ro...	684-5786
	874-4918
Smith Ronald...	628-5937
Smith Roog... PI	ADrndak 4-1307
Smith Roo?evelt ...Av	AUdbn 3-4999
Smith R... 42...	666-0174
Smith Rosa... ?RivDr	TO 2-8701
Smith Rosa... ?shAv	928-9112
Smith Rosab... 211?...151	AU 3-3697
Smith Rosale... ?Wa...	FO... ?187
Smith Rosamo... 3	?25
Smith Roscoe 2?Aud...	8-6773
Smith Rose 38?ntrlP...	9-1188
Smith Rose Mrs ?960 ...LOra...	?132
Smith Rose M... 5?22 ...ORegn	4?832
Smith Rose... 526W151	WA ?-8833
Smith Rose Lee 300W111	222-3361
Smith Rose M Mrs 2175 1Av	TR 6-6633
Smith Rose Marie 20W85	TR 7-9060
Smith Rose McGuire 433W21	CH 3-6706

Farmer Arthur W acctnt 50Brd	HA 2-2770
Farmer B 305E11	674-7874
Farmer Bea 28W131	281-6306
Farmer Capen 17W87	799-3658
Farmer Charlotte Mrs 20LaurlHlTer	928-3806
Farmer Don E 492 2Av	MU 6-6625
Farmer E S 225E63	355-0776
Farmer Eileen M 270W11	ORegn 5-5062
Farmer Elerf 2102AmstrdmAv	795-0201
Farmer Emma Mrs 2160MadAv	AUdbn 3-7982
Farmer Ernest	GRmrcy 3-8551
Farmer Ernestl... v	722-4263
Farmer F Malco... EEndAv	BU 8-2600
Farmer Fredd H... 8	?-4361
Farmer Fredk H... ?ay	?477
Farmer Geral...	
Farme...	
...J 217?arkAV	?-?99
Farmer John J 14 5Av	GR 5-3768
Farmer Laurence MD 24E82	RH 4-5577
Farmer Laurence MD ofc 107E85	BU 8-7774

dignitaries, such as Bishop and Abbott, were often given in jest as ironic nicknames to men in very different spheres of life, while the surname Parsons seems to have been used frequently for the parson's servants or relations or anyone domiciled "at the parson's." But the clerks, or lower orders of the clergy, were permitted to marry, and their numerous descendants are the truest representatives among us of medieval religion and learning.

These four occupational names are only a small sample of what can be found in the directory. All the typical figures of the Middle Ages are there: the knight, the squire, the page, the archer, and the harper; but none of English descent will be found whose craft or trade or office developed as late as 1400. There are Masons but no Bricklayers, Butchers but no Grocers, Tinkers but no Clockmakers, Painters but no Playwrights, not even a Soldier, for in the days when surnames were being formed, it was taken for granted that every man would fight for his feudal lord when the occasion arose.

Coming back to our list, we have three color names—Brown, White, and Green— all ranking very high in every English-speaking community, all good Old English monosyllables that were used as personal names or nicknames long before the Conquest. Brown and White represent the simple contrast of dark and fair, the darker type being rarer among the Anglo-Saxons and therefore more likely to be noticed. In this connection we may note that Schwartz, which means "black," is the commonest name of the fair-haired Germans in the Manhattan directory. White might imply old age, but was more often used for young men of strikingly blond coloring, as were many more picturesque expressions, such as Lillie, Swan, and Snow. At the time of the Conquest, White was already being used as a surname by several prominent Englishmen, as may be seen in a charter dated on the last day of Edward the Confessor's reign in which two of the witnesses are set down as Ordgar the White and Wulfwerd White, the latter being written without any article, exactly like a modern surname. At this date Brown was more often used as a Christian name, as Bruno still is in Italy. To make an affectionate diminutive of such a name the Saxons added their favorite ending, "-ing," which served many purposes. Browning might mean "the son of Brown" or "dear little Brown" or "good old Brown." Whiting, Manning, Harding, Gooding, and many others began in the same way, as familiar forms of Anglo-Saxon Christian names or nicknames.

Green is quite different from Brown and White. There is no doubt that very often it referred to a man's place of residence on "the village green." This is shown by the form in which the surname appears in early records, which is generally "atte grene," or at the green. But sometimes it is written "en le grene" (in the green), and then we are tempted to think of Jack-in-the-Green, or the Green Man, a figure dressed in leaves who featured in the springtime festival, typifying the return to life of the woods and linked with ancient fertility rites.

In this connection we should also consider the surname King, which, although it does not quite make the top twenty-five, comes close. Its origin has nothing to do with any real king or service to him. Looking through thirteenth-century tax rolls, one sees in village after village a peasant set down as Jack, or Hugh, or Walter "the king." This could only arise from some personification among the villagers that took place regularly, such as the choosing of a May King. By the nineteenth century the king had dropped out of this ceremony, leaving the principal part to a girl, but originally the central figure was a man. The name King may also come from the acting of miracle plays in which kings were portrayed, but this could not possibly account for its high numbers.

Other characters from early religious drama can be found in our directories, but in much smaller numbers. New York, for instance, has only fifty Angels to about nine hundred Kings, so that clearly a much more widespread origin must be found for the latter. I believe that it belongs to the May Day ceremonies and that many of the Greens do also.

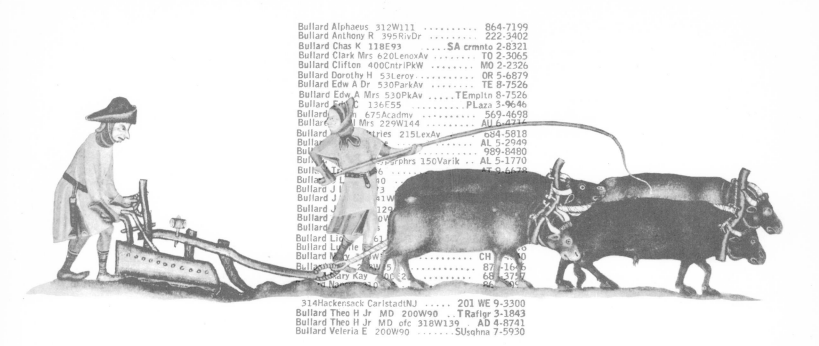

The remaining name on our list is Lee. Its numbers would not be so high without a contribution from the Chinese, but nonetheless it serves as a good representative of surnames of locality, being the most numerous of this class in England as well. Three other spellings, Lea, Ley, and Leigh, are derived from the same word, the Old English *lēah*, which meant at first a clearing in a wood, and later a stretch of grass that might be meadow or pasture or just the "village green" again, the center of communal life. As England was thickly forested in the days when the Angles and Saxons first invaded it, innumerable settlements began as mere clearings, and therefore "lea," as well as becoming a common name denoting such a location, also supplied the final syllable for hundreds of village names—Oakley, Ashley, Bradley (the broad lea), Stanley (the stony lea), and so forth. It is no wonder that it has made a common surname. In medieval rolls we often see it in such forms as "Simon atte lee," and occasionally the resulting surname retains the preposition, as in the case of Attlee, but this is exceptional. The Manhattan directory gives only four Attlees, six Atwells, and about thirty each of Atwoods and Atwaters; whereas the names Wells, Woods, and Waters appear in the hundreds. In France the normal development was to keep the preposition, giving such well-known names as Dubois and Dupont; but in England it usually dropped off.

Although we have only one name of locality on our top-scoring list—or one and a half, for Green is certainly one, in part—this category telling where a man lived is the largest of all English surname groups, but within it there is such a vast diversity of individual names that few of them are at all common. Naturally the most plentiful are the ordinary words like those just mentioned, Woods, Fields, Brooks, and so on; but when we begin to think of particular villages, hamlets, and farms from every part of England and Scotland, we are faced with literally thousands of separate surnames, many of them individually rare.

What does the possession of one of these village names imply? Certainly that its owner's ancestors lived in that spot for many generations. No one would acquire a village name without its being his real home, where his roots were deep, and this was probably before 1300. But whether your forebears were the principal owners and lords of the manor is a very hard thing to establish. The smaller the village the more likely it is to have been the case. In the first two centuries after the Conquest, the principal family in almost every village was known by the village's name, and younger sons seeking a livelihood elsewhere often took the name with them. Or, any man who had left his native place might be given its name as a surname, for such things were not done by any system but merely arose naturally in conversation. However,

it should be remembered that at the time when surnames were sticking in this way, the great majority of the peasantry were still bound in some sort of villein service and were not free to leave their birthplaces. Therefore a man called by the name of a village that he had left was more likely to be a son of its leading family, or at least a freeman, than one of the humbler villagers.

A surname from a larger place is clearly a different matter. If your name is Lincoln or Kent, all you can deduce from it is that your ancestors lived there at an early date, and that the name stuck to them when they left. Tax returns for London about the year 1300 include provincial surnames from every county in England.

Our eighteen leading English surnames have given us good samples of the four ways in which men acquired their names—from Christian names, occupations, descriptive nicknames, and places. But we have barely scratched the surface of a vast subject, which, when fully studied, can reveal endless details of the lives and habits of remote forebears.

The historian C. M. Matthews, whose married name is a patronymic from southern England, wrote English Surnames, *published last fall by Weidenfeld and Nicolson, London.*

The illustrations of medieval English occupations are from the fourteenth-century Luttrell Psalter, *now in the British Museum.*

FROM *Vachel Lindsay* BY EDGAR LEE MASTERS, SCRIBNER'S, 1935

Vachel Lindsay's Lost Weekend in Urbana

By M. M. MARBERRY

Urbana, Illinois, was no Sauk Centre, and my mother was no Carol Kennicott, but she did have a craving for culture and never missed the Chautauqua—including that memorable Saturday evening in 1922 when Vachel Lindsay came to perform. My father was dubious about spending twenty-five cents a ticket just to see a poet, but he gave in when mother pointed out that Lindsay also delivered temperance lectures. My parents were dry fanatics.

The turnout was surprisingly large, with some six hundred townspeople, faculty members, and college students attending. Everybody came to see a show, and Lindsay did not disappoint them. At first the students were in a challenging and derisive mood, but Lindsay quickly won them over, so much so that they became enthralled and cheered him after each reading just as they cheered when the Illinois football team scored a touchdown. The townspeople and the professors were less responsive. Some stared aghast at the poet, while others cradled their heads in embarrassment; none of them had seen a bona fide poet behave in such an outlandish manner. Lindsay's biographer, Elizabeth Ruggles, wrote that it was a unique experience to see him in the throes of a recital—his arms pumping up and down, his eyes rolling like a man in a fit, his body rocking, and his shoulders weaving. Her description was apt enough, for the auditorium was soon in a turmoil as Lindsay threw back his head, puffed out his chest, and began bellowing out his most spectacular and successful poem, "The Congo":

Fat black bucks in a wine-barrel room . . .
Beat an empty barrel with the handle of a broom,
*   Hard as they were able,*
*   Boom, boom,* BOOM,
With a silk umbrella and the handle of a broom,
Boomlay, boomlay, boomlay, BOOM*!*

Bounding to another part of the stage, Lindsay teetered back and forth on his heels, his hands jabbing the air, and, tipping his head back again, let go—slap, sock, and bang:

THEN I SAW THE CONGO, CREEPING THROUGH THE BLACK,
CUTTING THROUGH THE FOREST WITH A GOLDEN TRACK. . . .

Then along the riverbank
A thousand miles

Tattooed cannibals danced in files;
*   Then I heard the boom of the blood-lust song*
*   And a thigh-bone beating on a tin-pan gong. . . .*

Lindsay was accompanied throughout this recital by the tom-tom beat of a drum off stage. Suddenly the drum was silent and the poet lowered his voice and delivered the eerie last line in a menacing whisper:

Mumbo . . . Jumbo . . . will . . . hoo-doo . . . you.

After the seven minutes of gymnastics required to complete the poem, Lindsay was hoarse and dripping with sweat, and the audience was almost as exhausted. The windup brought the students to their feet roaring.

"The Congo" was the *pièce de résistance* of Vachel Lindsay's repertoire. He also recited "The Santa Fe Trail," "The Chinese Nightingale," "The Kallyope Yell," "General William Booth Enters into Heaven," "Abraham Lincoln Walks at Midnight," and "The Eagle That Is Forgotten," an elegy about Illinois' liberal governor, John P. Altgeld:

Sleep softly . . . eagle forgotten . . . under the stone.
Time has its way with you there, and the clay has its own.

The audience participated in the rendering of some poems, chanting from the printed program. In his "Daniel" the poet would cry out:

King Darius said to the lion:
"Bite Daniel. Bite Daniel.
"Bite him. Bite him. Bite him!"

and then the audience joined in:

THUS *roared the lion:*
"We want Daniel, Daniel, Daniel,
"We want Daniel, Daniel, Daniel,
"Grrrrrrrrrrrrrrrrrrrrrrrrrrrrrr."

It was an unforgettable night. The students felt they had seen the greatest theatrical act of the Urbana season. But the grownups had reservations about such a frenetic performance. They regarded Lindsay as a freak, not as a legitimate artist. To them it was like going to a slightly disreputable side show only faintly redeemed by a façade

Vachel Lindsay performing in 1928

of culture. My father's reaction was typical of the older generation: the poet had been undignified, prancing and scampering around like an acrobat. This "New Poetry" was pretty obscure stuff. A lot of shouting. Vachel Lindsay was certainly no Longfellow, no Whittier. What was the fellow trying to prove, anyway?

Lindsay could have told him. He thought of himself as an artistic originator whose "New Poetry" would, in short order, sweep all conventional forms of verse into the trash heap. As it turned out, he was wrong. Thirty-five years after Lindsay's death, his influence on modern poets is negligible. They admire his vivid imagery but shy clear of his chanted, syncopated rhythms, deplore his frequent alliteration, and regard him generally as an iambic curiosity.

Yet Lindsay *was* an innovator, though not, as he prophesied, in poetry. He was the first of the traveling troubadours to gain national attention. The Woody Guthries, the Bob Dylans, the Pete Seegers, and other minstrels owe him a debt for being the original voice of protest who performed on platforms before thousands, the man who smoothed the way for the horde of balladeers who today flourish from Berkeley to Princeton. But he is not revered by the current crowd, for they are not aware of his trail blazing, if indeed they know he ever existed.

Lindsay started out reciting protest verse—protest against the liquor traffic, against denial of the ballot to women—to the accompaniment of a stringed instrument, usually the guitar. Today these issues are academic, but platform protesting goes on, with the folk-rock singers using Lindsay's techniques to oppose the draft and the war in Vietnam.

At first Lindsay attracted little attention. Then, in 1913, as his poetic scope widened, he began intoning his verse in ragtime rhythm, in what he called "Higher Vaudeville" presentations. He was convinced that Americans "hate and abhor poetry," and so he sugar-coated the pill in order "to get the public." He developed a bouncy routine, totally unlike the ordinary, tame poetry reading; it was half revivalist and half jazz in style. He explained that his audiences thus were hoodwinked into thinking they were seeing a vaudeville act and were entertained. "And yet," Lindsay insisted, "I try to keep it to a real art." Lindsay's "New Poetry" caught on, his recitals became popular, and he made three successful cross-country tours. To see the poet striding and leaping about on the platform, gesticulating like a Billy Sunday gone mad and at the same time nasally chanting his verse to the tinkle of a guitar or the beat of a drum, was more than startling. Audiences everywhere were stunned, and Urbana was no exception.

Lindsay was scheduled to leave by train the morning after his performance, and was invited by the late Professor Stuart Pratt Sherman to stay overnight at his home. Sherman was well known on the campus as an essayist and a disciple of the Humanists, the literary and philosophical cult headed by Irving Babbitt and Paul Elmer More. I was

often in the Sherman home, since I was a friend of the professor's son John. The evening after the recital, I went over to John's house and was surprised to learn that Lindsay had missed the train. Professor Sherman had given him his ticket—transportation to Gilman, then a trip on the Illinois Central spur to Springfield—and yet he was still in bed! John told me that a few selected members of the faculty had been invited to the Sherman house after the reading, and that the poet had entertained them with what amounted to a repeat performance. A raspberry punch—nonalcoholic, of course—had been served, and as the evening wore on, the guest had become more and more exhilarated until finally he collapsed and had to be helped to bed. John and I were mystified. Surely Lindsay could not have been drunk—he was a temperance lecturer.

John said his parents were going out for dinner and asked me to stay around. When the Shermans came downstairs, they found us immersed in our schoolbooks. Mrs. Sherman said Mr. Lindsay was suffering from total exhaustion and was not to be disturbed. The professor looked apprehensive.

As soon as they had left, we threw aside our books, and a few minutes later we heard what we took to be the cries of a man in agony. We rushed up to the guest room and found Vachel Lindsay propped up in bed, wearing his long underwear and downing the contents of a half-pint bottle. Near at hand was a valise neatly stacked with more half-pints. The poet was in no pain. He merely had been reciting his verse.

Lindsay was affable enough, not at all resenting the intrusion on his privacy by a pair of teen-age boys. He motioned for us to sit down, opened another half-pint, and said he would recite to us. John closed the bedroom windows. Neighbors in Urbana had big ears.

Although at the time I regarded anyone over twenty-five as an old man, Vachel Lindsay struck me as being fairly young. No doubt I associated poets with youth, with Chatterton and Keats. I know now that he was forty-three. Anyway, he looked like a poet—and it is difficult to look like a poet when wearing long underwear. I remember to this day how tall and wraithlike he appeared, even though he was in bed. (Recently I came across Lindsay in a group photograph and found him to be, inexplicably, a rather chunky man of medium height.) He was blond, with a long, dangling forelock. His forehead was high, and a protruding lower lip gave him at times a slight pout. His enunciation was precise, his voice resonant—and loud. He would peer at you sharply from the corners of his eyes, without shifting his head. There was decidedly an air of wildness about him. That was the way I thought a poet should look.

We listened to Lindsay deliver his poems for almost two hours. He treated us like grownups, and we were enchanted with him.

John Sherman finally reminded me that his parents

would be back shortly. Before we left, I timidly mentioned an ambitious project I had been mulling over in my mind, one that would butter up my public-speaking teacher, who was showing a strong distaste for me. I asked Lindsay if he would read for twenty minutes or so to my eleventh-grade elocution class on the following morning at Urbana High School.

He agreed instantly. He even thanked me for the invitation, and said he was looking forward to the recital. I told him that the class met at eleven thirty and that I would pick him up at eleven. When we left, he saluted us with a gulp that emptied still another half-pint. He disposed of the empty as he had done before, tossing it across the room into an open closet, where it shattered. I have no idea what was in the bottles. Lindsay had mentioned that it was his favorite elixir. "Great as a tonic and bone hardener," he said solemnly.

At school the next day, my elocution teacher was delighted at the prospect of having Vachel Lindsay appear before her class. Then the thing got bigger. The principal heard the news and announced that the entire student body would gather in the school auditorium to hear the famous poet.

Promptly at eleven, I drove up to the Sherman residence in my Model T. I knew instinctively that the raffish Lindsay would enjoy riding to the school in a ramshackle machine that cost twenty dollars secondhand. As I approached the house, I could hear Lindsay singing upstairs. So could the neighbors, I noticed.

When Mrs. Sherman heard my story she was horrified. She said the poet was suffering from severe exhaustion, that he had not left his bed, that she was sending his meals upstairs, and that he could not possibly appear in public. She hustled me out of the house, instructing me, rather mysteriously I thought, to "say nothing about this to anyone."

I was too much of a coward to explain to the principal that Lindsay was not available. I simply stayed home. I learned later that the students, all eight hundred of them, had gathered in the auditorium and were happy about missing a whole class period. When I eventually saw the elocution teacher, I never mentioned the name of Vachel Lindsay, nor did she. But I flunked the course.

Before Lindsay left the Sherman household—a completely disrupted household, I now began to realize—I saw him twice again. I went to John's house Tuesday evening, and he told me that the poet was still staying on. The Shermans were waiting hopefully for their guest to leave; they were too genteel to boot him out. Mrs. Sherman was grim, her husband glum.

The fact of Lindsay's continued presence was kept a secret. He was isolated on the second floor, and the Shermans entertained no one. John told me that two college girls had come tripping up the sidewalk to keep an appointment with Professor Sherman, and that his mother had charged out of the house like a blocking halfback and shooed them off.

Later that evening John and I crept surreptitiously up the backstairs to visit our new friend. He was grumpy, not in the mood for singing or reciting. I noticed that his stock of half-pints had disappeared and that the litter of broken bottles in the closet had been carted away. This visit was not much fun for us. I felt as if I were visiting a man in the death cell.

Evidently Lindsay had forgotten altogether about appearing at the high school, for he did not mention it. In any event, our stay was cut short by Mrs. Sherman, who, when she heard voices in the guest room, bounded up the staircase and dragged us out, one on each hand. "He's still got his nervous trouble," Mrs. Sherman said. John walked halfway home with me and said his mother was upset because Lindsay had spent most of the night making long-distance calls, including a lengthy conversation with someone in Portland, Oregon.

I witnessed the eventual departure. Lindsay had arrived in town on Saturday, and he decided to leave Wednesday. The Shermans were dizzy with relief. As he was saying good-bye, Lindsay turned to me: "Don't forget about that date at the high school. I'm looking forward to it."

Lindsay was carrying his valise, obviously empty of bottles now, but the neck of a small bottle could be seen sticking out of his coat pocket. John told me he had seen Lindsay pouring cooking sherry from a jug he had found in the kitchen into a discarded bay-rum bottle. And later he told me that the poet had absent-mindedly walked off with a dozen of his father's silk socks.

The Shermans were beaming as they said their farewells, and Lindsay at long last walked out of the front door. There he paused. Undoubtedly he had suddenly recalled that Mrs. Sherman had prepared all his meals and served them to him in bed. He wanted to show he appreciated her hospitality. He reached around and patted her gently on the backside. Mrs. Sherman reeled with a horrified gasp. Then Lindsay said:

"The *coffee* was wonderful."

With that, Lindsay departed, and John and I never saw him again. The chances are the Shermans never did either.

Lindsay's farewell remark became a famous saying in Urbana. After a guest had dined particularly well, on a lavish five-course dinner, say, he would compliment the hostess with a casual, "The *coffee* was wonderful."

Vachel Lindsay's popularity as a platform balladeer continued for several years. His poetic powers had waned long before, for his most significant poems were all written before World War I. When the great depression struck, his day was over; people had no use for the frivolities of his "Higher Vaudeville." He was forgotten, just as he is forgotten today. In 1931 he died the hard way, swallowing lye.

M. M. Marberry, a free-lance writer living in New York, wrote "The Naked Lady" for the May, 1964, HORIZON.

ENGRAVING N.Y. PUB. LIB. PRINTS DIV.; DRAWINGS CHAS B SLACKMAN

SUMATRAN RHINOCEROS

JAVAN RHINOCEROS

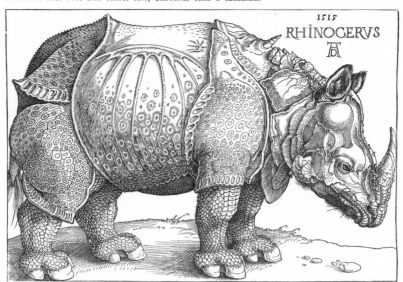

1515
RHINOCERVS

BLACK RHINOCEROS

WHITE RHINOCEROS

Albrecht Dürer's somewhat imaginative engraving of the Indian rhino, above, is surrounded by modern drawings of the other four species.

The Rhinoceros at Bay

CONTINUED FROM PAGE 20

wide, it lies along the south bank of the river. In a few minutes one has flown over it, en route to the nearest airport fifty miles beyond. But from a naturalist's point of view, this is one of the most important spots in all of eastern Asia.

A swampy and virtually roadless area, Kaziranga can be explored only from an elephant's back, which we found far superior to a Land-Rover or jeep: one feels a part of the landscape rather than an intrusion upon it. The magic hour is just after dawn. When we arose that first chill morning, a full moon hung on the western horizon. By the time we had mounted our elephant, the stars had faded and there was enough light to ford the shallow river near the entrance to the refuge. Guided by the mahout, who sits on the elephant's neck with his bare feet behind the animal's ears, our mount rolled like a destroyer in a rough sea as his feet sank in the mud of the river bottom; then he scrambled up the far bank and plunged into trackless grass that rose above our heads, dripping with dew. The heavy morning mist gave every object a two-dimensional quality. Individual trees stood out in

delicate silhouette; when a white egret alighted on the topmost branch of an acacia, one had the momentary illusion of an ink-wash painting from the brush of a Chinese master.

From somewhere in the swamp at our backs came the trumpeting of a wild elephant. Our elephant replied, and we took up the trail, finally coming on four black backs, humping up like whales in the sea of grass. The largest was a full-grown female elephant, who made a noisy but token charge at these intruders on her privacy; the smallest was a tiny calf, whose scars from a recent attack by a tiger explained his mother's touchiness.

Leaving the family in peace, we entered a broad swale of close-cropped grass at the center of which lay a shallow blue lake almost choked with water hyacinths. As the mist thinned, a group of dark-gray shapes became a herd of wild water buffalo, including one old bull with a huge spread of horns. The doglike figures scampering through the short grass were hog deer; farther off, shapely swamp deer watched us with more curiosity than fear, and a wild pig trotted along the edge of the lake. Suddenly, without warning, we came on our first rhino. Two thirds down in a mud wallow, he loomed out of the fog like a ship at

sea. As he clambered out on the drier ground, the illusion was strengthened by his coloring: battleship gray above, almost black below the water line, where the dark mud clung to his massive flanks. Head-on, with scrawny neck extended, upper lip curved like a beak, he reminded me of a huge snapping turtle; here was a true prehistoric monster rising from the swamps of a long-lost world.

Rhinos will occasionally charge an elephant, slashing with their razor-sharp teeth rather than using their horn; the rhino is, in fact, the only animal that will attack an elephant. Fortunately, the elephants in Kaziranga are trained to stand firm, and though we were within twenty yards of the rhino, we were in no immediate danger.

The amazing thing about the Indian rhino is his hide. Heavily folded, studded with rivetlike tubercles, it looks like armor plate, although actually it is easily cut and bleeds readily. The famous Indian naturalist E. P. Gee recounts the legend of how the rhino got its armor plating. "Once upon a time Lord Krishna decided to give up elephants as battle animals, and to use the rhino, because mahouts were too easy a target for enemy archers. So a rhino was captured, dressed in armor, and trained. But when the animal was brought before Lord Krishna, it was found that it was too stupid to learn and obey orders, so it was driven back to the forest—with its armor still on it." As a matter of fact, Gee continues, "rhino were actually used by some of the old kings in India as front-line 'tanks' in warfare. They had iron tridents fixed to their horns. . . ."

Presently seven rhinos were in sight, dotted around the open grassland. One of them stood mooselike in the shallow water, his face whiskered from a mouthful of aquatic plants. A large heron, reminiscent of our Great Blue, lit at the water's edge, near a raft of Brahmany ducks. A flock of long-tailed green parrots flew overhead with raucous shrieks. And now in the distance emerged the perfect background to this dreamlike scene: the long, jagged range of the Himalayas, white towers against a pale-blue sky.

To see the Indian rhino in such a setting is worth a hundred theoretical arguments for wildlife conservation— just as an hour among the redwoods will convince the most practical man that a tree may be worth more alive than dead. The poachers, however,

are immune to the conservationists' arguments; to them, a dead rhino can be worth a lifetime's honest wages. Not long ago a rich Indian who fell ill in London sent home for the blood of a freshly killed rhino, just as men in the Middle Ages sought unicorn blood to heal their wounds. Generally, however, rhino blood is not in great demand; most poachers merely saw off the horns and leave the bodies to rot.

A census of the rhinos in Kaziranga, conducted in March, 1966, by a scientist from Johns Hopkins University and a team of two hundred Indians, came up with a total figure of three hundred and sixty-six. During the two years prior to our visit, twenty-four animals had been killed by poachers. For a slow-breeding species (one calf every three years), this is a dangerous rate of attrition. Only the strictest methods of protecting—such as those employed in the white rhino reserves of Natal—can save it.

Wherever he still exists, the rhino is at bay. The two African species will probably win through, provided the African governments maintain the parks and reserves. In Asia the Sumatran rhino, which so impressed Marco

Polo, has all but disappeared within a single generation, perhaps to join in oblivion the other species of animals that are becoming extinct, through man's agency, at the rate of more than one a year. The Javan rhino may endure for a while in the fastnesses of his remote peninsula. The Great Indian, despite continued depredations, has a chance of survival in the refuges set aside for it.

In a wholly tamed and manicured world there would be no room for the rhinoceros; he would become as much of an anachronism as did the unicorn in the age of reason. Yet to those who need what Henry Thoreau called "the tonic of wildness," the rhino's great horn, not in a powder but firmly planted on his living, breathing nose, is worth more than its weight in gold.

Meanwhile, as the rhino becomes scarcer, the actual market price of his horn goes up. His supposed contribution to the art of love has become the greatest threat to his existence. He is battling for life against a legend.

Paul Brooks has written several articles about wildlife for HORIZON. *A dedicated conservationist, he is Editor-in-Chief of Houghton Mifflin.*

STATEMENT OF OWNERSHIP, MANAGEMENT, AND CIRCULATION (Act of October 23, 1962; Section 4369, Title 39, U.S. Code)

1. Date of filing: October 1, 1966
2. Title of Publication: HORIZON
3. Frequency of Issue: quarterly
4. Location of known office of publication: 551 Fifth Ave., City, County, and State of New York, 10017
5. Location of the headquarters or general business offices of the publishers: 551 Fifth Ave., N.Y., N.Y., 10017
6. Names and Addresses of Publisher, Editor, and Managing Editor: Publisher, James Parton, 551 Fifth Ave., N.Y., N.Y., 10017; Editor: Joseph J. Thorndike, 551 Fifth Ave., N.Y., N.Y., 10017; Managing Editor: Charles L. Mee, Jr., 551 Fifth Ave., N.Y., N.Y., 10017
7. Owner: American Heritage Publishing Co., Inc., 551 Fifth Ave., N.Y., N.Y., 10017. Names and addresses of stockholders owning or holding 1 per cent or more of total amount of stock of American Heritage Publishing Co., Inc.: American Association for State and Local History, Nashville, Tenn.; The Society of American Historians, Inc., c/o Prof. Eric F. Goldman, Dept. of History, Princeton University, Princeton, N.J.; Charles Bruce Catton, Irwin Glusker, Oliver O. Jensen, Frank H. Johnson, Richard M. Ketchum, James Parton, individually and as Trustee under Declarations of Trust for James Parton III, for Dana Parton, for Nike Parton, and for Agnes L. Parton and a Child of the Grantor, Joseph J. Thorndike, individually and as Trustee under Declaration of Trust for Alan Thorndike, all of 551 Fifth Ave., N.Y., N.Y.; Virginia L. Thorndike, 520 E. 77th St., N.Y., N.Y.; Gerald P. Rosen, Game Cock Island, Byram, Conn.; Merrill, Lynch, Pierce, Fenner & Smith, Inc.,* 70 Pine Street, N.Y., N.Y.; Alexander Hehmeyer, 575 Madison Ave., N.Y., N.Y.; Arnold H. Maremont, 168 N. Michigan Ave., Chicago,

Ill.; Roger S. Phillips, P.O. Box 11, Rowayton, Conn.; Shearson Hammill & Co.,† 14 Wall Street, N.Y., N.Y.; E. J. Stackpole, 220 Telegraph Bldg., Harrisburg, Pa.; Barbara Joan Straus, c/o Irving Trust Co., 1 Wall St., N.Y., N.Y.; John Thorndike, 11 Owenoke, Westport, Conn.; Evans & Co., Inc., 60 Wall St., N.Y., N.Y.

*Held for account of clients, no one of whom is believed to own or hold 1 per cent or more of total amount of stock.
†Held for account of clients, one of whom, Dell Publishing Co., Inc., 750 Third Ave., N.Y., N.Y., is believed to own or hold 1 per cent or more of total amount of stock.

8. Known bondholders, mortgagees, and other security holders owning or holding 1 per cent or more of total amount of bonds, mortgages, or other securities: None.
9. Paragraphs 7 and 8 include, in cases where the stockholder or security holder appears upon the books of the company as trustee or in any other fiduciary relation, the name of the person or corporation for whom such trustee is acting; also the statements in the two paragraphs show the affiant's full knowledge and belief as to the circumstances and conditions under which stockholders and security holders who do not appear upon the books of the company as trustees, hold stock and securities in a capacity other than that of a bona fide owner. Names and addresses of individuals who are stockholders of a corporation which itself is a stockholder or holder of bonds, mortgages, or other securities of the publishing corporation have been included in paragraphs 7 and 8 when the interests of such individuals are equivalent to 1 per cent or more of the total amount of the stock or securities of the publishing corporation.
10. THIS ITEM MUST BE COMPLETED FOR ALL PUBLICATIONS EXCEPT THOSE WHICH DO NOT CARRY

ADVERTISING OTHER THAN THE PUBLISHER'S OWN AND WHICH ARE NAMED IN SECTIONS 132.231, 132.-232, and 132.233, POSTAL MANUAL (Sections 4355a, 4355b, and 4356 of Title 39, U.S. Code).

	Average No. Copies Each Issue During Preceding 12 Months	Single Issue Nearest to Filing Date
A. Total No. Copies Printed (Net Press Run)	156,000	159,000
B. Paid Circulation		
1. Sales through dealers and carriers, street vendors, and counter sales	700	800
2. Mail Subscriptions	147,200	149,900
C. Total Paid Circulation	147,900	150,700
D. Free Distribution (including samples) by mail, carrier, or other means	2,100	1,500
E. Total Distribution (Sum of C and D)	150,000	152,200
F. Office Use, Leftover, Unaccounted, Spoiled After Printing	6,000	6,800
G. Total (Sum of E and F—should equal net press run shown in A)	156,000	159,000

I certify that the statements made by me above are correct and complete.

James Parton
Publisher

I don't think I would have realized what was happening in the world of furs if there had not been an initial element of fear. Last winter on Fifth Avenue I began to see things coming toward me that I thought had escaped from the zoo. This is no mere joke—in fact, it's no joke at all. By a quirk of realty, New York's Central Park Zoo is only half a dozen blocks from the axis of high fashion, 57th Street and Fifth Avenue, where our most elegant ladies go in and out of our most elegant shops: so near that we New Yorkers can often hear, even in our perpetual haste, even above our perpetual din, the roar of a lion or the bark of a seal or the howl of a cheetah. More than most city dwellers, we know that real animal skins, with real animals in them, are never more than a few fast bounds away.

True, most Americans don't have this particular problem. But all of us have seen enough B movies about the African jungle to be scared, almost out of our own skins, by the sight of an approaching pelt, especially if it is so big and bulky that we have no way of knowing, or any reason to suspect, that there is a girl inside. Who can resist that instinctive sense of danger, that momentary stab of fear? Not me.

This, in brief, is how I first learned about the arrival of "fun furs," and I'm glad I found out what they are. Now that winter is here again, I can walk along the avenue without flinching at the sight of an approaching Bengal tiger or Siamese leopard, Arctic wolf or Alaskan lynx, secure in the knowledge that it is only Baby Jane Holzer or Mrs. Larry Rivers. Of course it's possible that some day a Bengal tiger or a Siamese leopard really will escape from the zoo, and I'll discover the hard way that it is not Baby Jane Holzer or Mrs. Larry Rivers. But meanwhile, if fun furs are here, I'm going to have fun looking at them.

And part of the fun is knowing that the gaudy new pelts have largely replaced mink, at least for the time being —and that's the only time that counts in matters of personal finance. Mink is one fur that I don't have any trouble

PLEASE DON'T FEED THE FUN FURS

By WILLIAM K. ZINSSER

recognizing. It's that sleek brown stuff that glides out of limousines and luxury apartments, looking like a million dollars, or, at any rate, five thousand—a constant reminder of American free enterprise at its fattest and my bank account at its thinnest.

Luckily, my wife has never wanted a mink coat, but I thought that she might enjoy a fun possum or a fun badger, and that with a bit of fiscal prudence— that is, a loan from my fun banker—I might be able to get one. Here, however, I ran into a language barrier that almost stopped me. Where at first I had heard the new pelts described as "fun furs," I now began to see advertisements referring to them as the "second fur."

This was bad. It meant that my wife couldn't have a second fur until she had a first fur—i.e., mink or sable. Does anyone buy a second car until he has a first car worthy of his station? Or a second house until he is established in a first house that is bigger and better? In America today, the word "second" means that a person is rich enough to be pretentious before he can be himself.

It means having enough money to buy a Cadillac before plunging on that kicky little red convertible, to buy an apartment on Park Avenue before building that darling little house on the

dunes. "Second" means what it says: it comes after first. My wife was doomed to roam the streets in monkey or civet, cheetah or skunk, living a lie. "How amusing," people would say of her second fur, certain that her first fur was ready at home for the opera. Which it wasn't going to be—my fun banker isn't *that* much fun.

I decided to seek counseling, as the advice columns in newspapers say when they mean psychotherapy. But for my counselor I chose Jacques Kaplan, the furrier who claims to have started the new trend. I couldn't have chosen a better doctor.

"Mink went out as a status symbol fifteen years ago," he said. "Women decided it was in bad taste to wear mink as a way of showing off their wealth, and sales fell sharply. In 1947 the total sales of furs in this country were $475,000,000, and by 1964 they were down to $260,000,000—quite a drop, because during this same period the gross national product quadrupled.

"That's why I decided to de-emphasize fur as a luxury and make it just something warm and wonderful that could be worn at the supermarket or anywhere else. My first 'fun fur' was guanaco, which is a llama from Peru, and that was a big hit. Since then I've introduced all kinds of new furs, and so have other designers. As a result, last year's fur sales went up 25 per cent over the year before, and this year the increase will be even greater. Furs are finally 'in' because they're not an icon any more—they're tongue-in-cheek."

He showed me a roomful of furs that

DRAWINGS BY CHAS B SLACKMAN

definitely were not icons, their colors bright, their shapes surprising. There was the guanaco that started it all. There was lynx and leopard, otter and ocelot, jaguar and jackal, monkey and mole, skunk and squirrel, tiger and zebra. There was rabbit dyed to look like civet and rabbit dyed to look like fox. (Evidently anything looks more expensive than rabbit.) There was a coat made of white mink-paws, and another of kangaroo, and another of genet. "I saw that at a zoo in the Pyrenees," Mr. Kaplan explained. "As a matter of fact, I got a lot of these ideas while taking my children to zoos when they were younger."

All the coats looked, if not exactly like mink, at least respectable, even the lowly weasel. "Ten years ago if you gave your wife a five-hundred-dollar fur coat she would have resented it," Mr. Kaplan said. "She would have preferred a mink stole—which is what a bad one would cost. Today most women would rather have a good fun fur coat than a bad section of mink."

"You mean," I asked, "that my wife could own a second fur before she had a first fur?"

"Sure," he said, and I knew that I was on to something big. It was a breakthrough in the whole concept of second items coming second. Now I could get a second boat (rowboat) before a first boat (cabin cruiser), or a second dog (mongrel) before a first dog (poodle). New visions of social acceptability began to swim before my eyes.

"It used to be," Mr. Kaplan explained, "that fashion came from the top. If the Duchess of Windsor wore a new style, every midinette in Paris and every salesgirl in Chattanooga wanted it. Affluence was status. Today taste comes up from below. The Beatles had a big influence on style. So did the black-leather motorcycle crowd—that's where the 'hard look' of Courrèges came from. Today's patterned stockings grew out of those scruffy black stockings that Beatnik girls wore in Greenwich Village. You notice it in new dance forms, too—like the frug. Rich people get bored with the same

old stuff and start looking for kicks."

This was another breakthrough. Now I wouldn't need to wait around, every fall, to see what the Duke of Windsor had selected for the season. Perhaps I could even set a new style myself. My daily writer's garb, so long in derision—the frayed shirts, rumpled khakis, and torn sneakers—might well work their way up to Savile Row and be featured in *Tailor & Cutter*.

That would take care of my own status, but what about my wife's? "Tell me," I said to Mr. Kaplan, "when mink went out as a status symbol, what took its place?"

"Culture," he said. "Owning good art, going to the ballet, hearing fine music—all that."

Well, heaven knows I've heard enough about the "culture boom," and I know that "cultural centers" are

springing up like motels. But I never dreamed that culture would replace mink—it was positively un-American. It was also positively expensive. Would I now be expected to bring home an occasional Matisse or a Flemish tapestry or a Benin bronze, to buy a season box at the Metropolitan Opera, to hold a series of little dinners for Samuel Barber and Allen Ginsberg?

I was more muddled than ever. Having sought counsel on the changing status of fur, I was now faced with the changing status of status itself. Where could a family jump into the moving stream with any confidence of

being in the right place at the right moment? Perhaps if I stalled for time, the art boom would run its course. Every Picasso, every T'ang vase, every George III teapot, would finally be bought by museums and millionaires and put beyond popular reach.

"When culture goes out as a status symbol," I said to Mr. Kaplan, "what will take its place?"

"I think I know," he said, "but the change won't occur for several years."

"Why will it take so long?" I asked.

"Well, there are always certain people who set the styles, and it takes the rest of the country a while to catch up. In the case of the fun furs, certain women have been wearing them for a number of years—girls like, say, Baby Jane Holzer and Mrs. Larry Rivers— and at last they are being copied by rich ladies who were too conservative to wear them before. This winter you'll see fun furs everywhere. So naturally the stylesetters are getting bored, and they're beginning to turn to the style that will be the most 'in' a couple of years from now."

"And what's that?" I asked.

"Mink," he said.

Mink dressed in mink

Water
of
Life

Tested with a glowing splint under favorable conditions, the breath of a habitual whisky drinker will light with a pop and burn with a blue flame; it will also discolor paint, shrivel foliage, rot delicate fabrics, and asphyxiate a swarm of bees. I mention these facts simply to attract attention and not from a love of the sensational. Whisky marches under a variety of flags or banners, copiously advertised, so that words like "Scotch," "Irish," "Bourbon," and "Rye," which once had distinct and useful meanings of their own, are now little more than signals to alcoholics. Although it can be made in a bath with the aid of a kettle, whisky —which may alternatively be spelled w-h-i-s-k-e-y—is normally produced by means of a pot still or a patent still. The relative merits of the whiskies distilled in one or the other of these pieces of apparatus are the subject of *prolonged, repeated, and very tedious argument among those who claim to "know about whisky." The real differences are small, and those which are discussed are largely imaginary. (Ask such a debater to draw diagrams of a pot still and a patent still; his inability to do so may persuade him to change the subject.)* This is not to say that all whiskies are equal. Age is of some importance. If whisky is matured in wooden casks for several years, some of the more quickly acting poisons may be leached out, precipitated, or decomposed. This process also serves to impart the characteristic and encouraging color to whiskies which may have emerged from the still quite colorless— and therefore visually indistinguishable from gin, vodka, or water. Should it fail to do so, the manufacturer will not scruple to color the whisky with caramelized sugar.

Setting aside all these trivia, I can now summarize the characteristics of this undeniably important fluid.

Definition: A spirit distilled from malted barley or other grain (*Concise Oxford Dictionary*). Note that it is not described as "good to drink" or even "fit for human consumption." In this, as in other ways, it resembles sulphuric acid.

Etymology: The name "whisky" is derived from the Gaelic *"uisge beatha,"* meaning "water of life," a designation which can hardly be anything but ironic.

Color: More or less yellow, the color associated with bile, jaundice, anxiety, envy, jealousy, cowardice, treachery, and decay.

Taste and Smell: Nauseating; offensive to the mucous membranes.

Other Properties: Inflammable; can be used as fuel for spirit lamps. A good solvent for varnish and shellac. Germicide. Occasionally used for maturing tobacco pipes and cleaning windows.

Effects on Human Body: Taken internally, whisky separates the nerve endings and produces a short-lived exhilaration. This is quickly succeeded by dizziness, partial to total loss of balance, nausea, retching, vomiting, complete loss of muscular control, and coma. On recovering consciousness the normal symptoms are violent headaches, biliousness, liverishness, intense thirst, lassitude, and bad breath. Prolonged dosing over many years gradually mortifies the tissues and the mind, brings madness and premature death.

Methods of Introduction: Many people like to take whisky neat to get the ordeal over as quickly as possible. Others, less sensitive, prefer it diluted. The most common vehicles for dilution are water and soda water, but ginger ale and sweet vermouth are also used from time to time. There are cases on record of whisky having been drunk with such diluents as tonic water (in mistake for soda), port, coffee, milk, honey, and lemon juice. Oddly enough, it is seldom injected directly into the blood stream.

It would, I suppose, be unfair to pass judgment on whisky and its consumers without hearing a defense of some sort. But what defense can there be? What would the articulate whisky drinker hoarsely mutter? Something like this, perhaps:

"Whisky is golden. Whisky is the elixir of happiness, the softener of sorrow, the easer of pain; a tonic, a stimulant, the fountainhead of conviviality and the harbinger of revelry. *It tides the sick over crises, fires the wounded with a will to live, transmutes cowardice to bravery. Whisky is sunlight to friendship and moonshine to love, lighting with laughter the seamed face, freeing the tongue tied by fear, evoking the improbable story and hilarious applause. See the men smilingly grouped about their golden glasses; their expanding spheres of benevolence intersect, comrades for the nonce.* After the party, homeward bound, the giggling pedestrian assuredly steps, the rosy motorist laughingly swerves. Stretched in bed, the feet perpetually rise, delightful delusion. Memories of jokes cracked renew laughter, sleepy now and slower. Nip from plated flask brings courage to maiden speaker, fortifies traveler plodding through snowdrifts. Revenue to benign government, profit to philanthropic manufacturer, living to open-hearted publican. Whisky, golden panacea, bottled wonder-worker."

Fergus Allen drinks his whisky in England. He has written for Atlantic Monthly *and various British magazines.*

By FERGUS ALLEN